110301

OXFORD WORLD'S CLASSICS

DISCOURSE ON THE ORIGIN OF
INEQUALITY

JEAN-JACQUES ROUSSEAU (1712–78) was born in Geneva, at that time an independent republic of which Rousseau would proudly call himself a citizen. His mother, Suzanne Bernard, died soon after his birth. His father, Isaac Rousseau, a watchmaker, left Geneva when his son was 10, leaving his son in the care of relatives. In 1728 Rousseau decided to seek his fortune elsewhere. He served as domestic in a prominent Turin family, but he found a new home in Chambéry with Mme de Warens, who acted by turns as his mother, mentor, and lover. He taught himself philosophy and literature, worked briefly as a tutor in Lyons, and in 1742 arrived in Paris, where he met Diderot and Condillac, as well as Thérèse Levasseur, his lifelong companion. After the success of his *Discourse on the Sciences and the Arts* (1750), which criticized the corrupting influence of civilization, he resigned his position as secretary in the wealthy Dupin family and from then on supported himself by his pen, although he continued to enjoy the hospitality of enlightened aristocrats. He wrote articles on music and political economy for Diderot's *Encyclopaedia*, and an opera, *The Village Soothsayer*. The *Discourse on Inequality* appeared in 1755, and a polemical *Letter to d'Alembert on Stage-performances* in 1758.

Rousseau's novel *Julie, or the New Héloïse* (1761), was greeted enthusiastically, but the *Social Contract*, his boldest political work, and his treatise on education, *Émile* (both 1762), were condemned as subversive. Fleeing arrest, Rousseau travelled in Switzerland, where he began his autobiographical *Confessions* (published posthumously), to England at the invitation of David Hume, and back to the French provinces, where, his mind increasingly troubled, he lived under a pseudonym. He was allowed to return to Paris in 1770, where he composed his *Reveries of the Solitary Walker*. He died at Ermenonville outside Paris in 1778.

FRANKLIN PHILIP is a translator and lives in Boston. In 1989 he won the Translation Prize of the French-American Foundation for *The Statue Within: An Autobiography* by François Jacob, and he has translated many other works from the French, including *The End of the Soviet Empire: The Triumph of the Nations* by Hélène Carrère d'Encausse (1993).

PATRICK COLEMAN is Professor of French at the University of California at Los Angeles, and author of *Rousseau's Political Imagination* (Geneva, 1984).

D1630764

OXFORD WORLD'S CLASSICS

*For over 100 years Oxford World's Classics have brought
readers closer to the world's great literature. Now with over 700
titles—from the 4,000-year-old myths of Mesopotamia to the
twentieth century's greatest novels—the series makes available
lesser-known as well as celebrated writing.*

*The pocket-sized hardbacks of the early years contained
introductions by Virginia Woolf, T. S. Eliot, Graham Greene,
and other literary figures which enriched the experience of reading.
Today the series is recognized for its fine scholarship and
reliability in texts that span world literature, drama and poetry,
religion, philosophy and politics. Each edition includes perceptive
commentary and essential background information to meet the
changing needs of readers.*

OXFORD WORLD'S CLASSICS

JEAN-JACQUES ROUSSEAU

Discourse on the Origin of Inequality

Translated by
FRANKLIN PHILIP

Edited with an Introduction and Notes by
PATRICK COLEMAN

OXFORD
UNIVERSITY PRESS

OXFORD
UNIVERSITY PRESS

Great Clarendon Street, Oxford OX2 6DP

Oxford University Press is a department of the University of Oxford.
It furthers the University's objective of excellence in research, scholarship,
and education by publishing worldwide in

Oxford New York

Athens Auckland Bangkok Bogotá Buenos Aires Calcutta
Cape Town Chennai Dar es Salaam Delhi Florence Hong Kong Istanbul
Karachi Kuala Lumpur Madrid Melbourne Mexico City Mumbai
Nairobi Paris São Paulo Singapore Taipei Tokyo Toronto Warsaw

with associated companies in Berlin Ibadan

Oxford is a registered trade mark of Oxford University Press
in the UK and in certain other countries

Published in the United States
by Oxford University Press Inc., New York

Translation © Franklin Philip 1994
Editorial material © Patrick Coleman 1994

British Library Cataloguing in Publication Data

Data available

Library of Congress Cataloging in Publication Data

Discourse on the origin of inequality / Jean-Jacques Rousseau ;
translated by Franklin Philip ; edited with an introduction by
Patrick Coleman
Includes bibliographical references.
1. Equality.   2. Natural law.   3. Political science.
I. Title.   II. Series.
JC179.R814   1994   320'.01'1—dc20   93–17535

ISBN 0-19-283981-0

3 5 7 9 10 8 6 4 2

Printed in Great Britain by
Clays Ltd, St Ives plc

CONTENTS

INTRODUCTION

THE *Discourse on the Origin and Foundations of Inequality among Men*, Rousseau's first major philosophical work, was published in 1755, at the floodtide of the French Enlightenment. In a concentrated, provocative argument, Rousseau pursues—and at the same time questions—some of the central ambitions of early modern thought: to define the distinctive characteristics of humanity through a comparative analysis of the ways men live in various kinds of groups and geographical environment around the world; to offer a rational, secular account of human development in history, from a 'natural' state common to all to highly differentiated societies; and to provide a common standard for judging the legitimacy of political institutions in an era beginning to recognize religious and national diversity.

In no other of his books does Rousseau refer more widely and more approvingly to the work of his contemporaries. At the end of the preceding decade, Montesquieu had produced his vast enquiry into *The Spirit of the Laws*; the philosopher Condillac had confidently extended Locke's work on the origin of human knowledge; Buffon, the most eminent French scientist of the age, had issued the first instalments of his multi-volume *Natural History*. In 1751 Rousseau's friend Diderot, together with the mathematician d'Alembert, had launched the monumental *Encyclopaedia*, designed not only as a repository of knowledge but as a vehicle for social improvement and political reform. These works, and beyond them the work of the seventeenth-century natural rights philosophers, provide the immediate context for Rousseau's investigation into the basis of social institutions. Yet, as the title suggests, improvement and happy consensus are not the focus of Rousseau's work. Throughout his account of civilization's advances, he lays constant stress on the disparities in men's status and power and on pervasive distortions in

The surnames in parentheses refer to entries in the Select Bibliography below.

the methods used to justify—indeed, aggravate—inequality.

Despite his disenchanted view of progress, Rousseau was determined, nevertheless, to provide an account of human development his readers would find reasonable and which would stimulate their desire for reform. The tension between the author's pessimism and his desperate hope gives the work a particular force and an enduring fascination. For two hundred years readers have been stirred by its passionate analysis of the patterns of oppression and by the two alternative images it evokes: the vivid depiction of men living isolated but free and independent lives in the state of nature, and the dimmer but no less seductive prospect of 'revolutions' that might bring governments closer to their legitimate form. Rousseau's ambivalent account of 'natural' man's fall into self-consciousness was echoed by poets in the Romantic era and beyond. The problematic link he established between human 'perfectibility' and inequality of rights challenged Kant and other philosophers to explain the detours and contradictions of progress. According to Marx's colleague Friedrich Engels, the *Discourse* anticipated a materialist dialectic in its interplay of positive and negative moments, although it fell short of discovering the real dynamic of history. For Claude Lévi-Strauss, on the other hand, it is precisely because Rousseau is so reluctant to smooth over 'the passage from nature to culture' that the *Discourse on Inequality* may properly be called 'the first anthropological treatise in French literature'.

While the paradoxical quality of the *Discourse* has always been part of its appeal, it has also provoked a debate about the work's intention and internal coherence as well as some persistent misunderstandings. Rousseau has been thought to extol the peaceful life of the 'noble savage', even though his state of nature is devoid of moral attributes and shadowed by sudden death. He has been seen as condemning all civilization as oppressive, and yet not only does he finally accept the need for some social inequality, but he expresses a fierce loyalty to his native city, the small republic of Geneva. Rousseau denounces the alienation of freedom in all political societies, but he praises a state known for its thoroughly regulated way of life. It is true that the myth of the noble savage has been discredited, and that in more recent years critics have been more willing to grant that apparent contradictions in the text may stem from Rousseau's tendency to mix theoretical boldness with practical caution. Yet, even sympathetic critics still disagree in their approach to the text. For some, Rousseau's fondness for paradox and other rhetorical flourishes makes it necessary to pick and choose among the various parts of the *Discourse* in order to reconstruct a worthy philosophical argument (Hall). For others, everything in the text is worthy of consideration because ultimately expressive of a personality whose very idiosyncrasies offer important insights into the psychology of modern humanity (Starobinski). Another kind of approach views the sometimes awkward relation between theoretical and practical considerations, or between Rousseau's thought and his style, as itself a matter of political import. The text's complications may be strategic, enabling Rousseau to address a diverse public consisting of casual, unreflective readers looking for comfort or easy answers and those, much less numerous, who have the ability and patience to read between the lines (Masters; Rousseau, ed. Meier). What looks like a strategy may, on the contrary, derive not from a controlling intention but from a structural necessity in the text itself, from metaphors and narrative forms that in Rousseau are inseparable from the definition of the most abstract ideas (Derrida, de Man).

These difficulties of interpretation focus on what may be called the rhetorical dimension of the text. Rhetoric can refer to the external orientation of an argument or the figures of speech employed within it, and both these aspects of the *Discourse* have attracted increasing interest in recent years. Indeed, this particular work of Rousseau's is now prized as much for its methodological interest as for the specific usefulness of its historical or political ideas. Rousseau would not, perhaps, be disappointed by this turn of events. According to the *Discourse* itself, one of his primary concerns was to illustrate the difficulty of knowing that most elusive object of study, man. Each of the approaches outlined above has contributed to a greater appreciation of the issues involved in Rousseau's text, and of its distinctive style. To understand the thrust of Rousseau's rhetoric, however, we must beware of splitting it off too much from its context. That context is not only a vague background of circumstances. Nor is it a single determining force pushing it in one direction. Rather, the context of an essay in political persuasion such as Rousseau's may be thought of as the intersection of a variety of discourses taken up and transformed by an author who must, none the less, adopt the vocabulary available to him or her (Baker, Pocock). The circumstances in which authors write are not simply the social conditions they want to address; they include forms of address that channel—that is, enable and constrain—communication.

It is especially important—and particularly difficult—to keep this in mind when reading the works of the French Enlightenment. Writers in eighteenth-century France were cut off from participation in political life, and what intellectual debate about political issues did take place was often distorted by censorship. The deepening paralysis of potentially oppositional forces like the *parlements* or reforming segments of the upper classes, caught between their privileges and the uncertain benefits of reform, made it extremely difficult to articulate any clear relation between theory and practice. And yet, the France of the *ancien régime* was not a systematically authoritarian state. In the salons of the social élite where the *philosophes* found a welcome, as well as in the private but often extensive circulation of letters and manuscripts, there was opportunity to display boldness of wit and philosophical speculation. In his analysis of the causes of the Revolution, Tocqueville with some justification criticized the polarized, abstract quality of the *philosophes*' plans for reform, but our own understanding of the period has sometimes taken on some of the same abstract quality. This is perhaps especially true of Rousseau, who insisted on the uniqueness and autonomy of his work. Without denying his originality, we should include in our definition of his intention the different ways in which the *Discourse* reconfigures its contexts.

From the beginning, Rousseau defined himself by his oppositional stance. His first book, the *Discourse on the Sciences and the Arts* (1750), articulated a sense of indignation, a conviction that something in civilization was radically wrong. If, as Marx observed, humanity at any moment in history only sets itself tasks it can hope to solve, Rousseau calls attention to what has to be left aside when measuring success. Displaced by family circumstances from Geneva's independent artisan class and making his way in the polite world of the French capital, Rousseau was always conscious of ideals and identities abandoned along the way. In 1756, a year after the *Discourse on Inequality* was published, he would in fact leave Paris for the countryside and proclaim his desire to write more authentically, for himself. This gesture was intended to mark the recovery of his independence, but it was complicated if not contradicted by the fact that Rousseau was going to live on the wealthy Mme d'Épinay's estate. Similarly, Rousseau's first discourse defined his opposition to the consensus of polite society much more clearly than it did the point of view from which he wrote.

The problem was that Rousseau could not simply reject the dominant spirit of the Enlightenment. One of the *philosophes*' essential principles was the independent critique of traditional authority. Rousseau might appeal to the stable wisdom of the ancients, but his own career, the path of social and intellectual mobility through which he gained a reputation as an individual talent, marks him as a modern man. And, as he was well aware, nostalgia for the simple life is itself a byproduct of advancing civilization. Indeed, it was thanks to his brilliant assaults on wit and learning that Rousseau had first won acclaim in Paris. The *Discourse on the Sciences and the Arts* was written for an essay competition established by the Academy of Dijon. The topic was whether intellectual and economic progress had contributed to the moral improvement of humanity. With a wealth of literary allusion, Rousseau had argued that the arts destroyed virtue. The force of his paradoxical rhetoric won him the prize. It has been pointed out that his success may be attributed in part to the particular character of the Academy:

an association of local notables professedly devoted to learning and social polish, but at the same time resentful of the
more glamorous and cosmopolitan élite from which they felt
excluded. Rousseau's essay gave the academicians both a
means of gaining widespread publicity and a vocabulary in
which they and many others could express their discomfort
with a society that made publicity so important.

Not that the words Rousseau used were themselves new:
he drew on such traditional sources as Plato, the history of
republican Rome, and the sceptical essays of Montaigne. But
these works pre-dated the scientific revolution of Galileo and
Newton. Old suspicions regarding the certainty of knowledge or the desirability of its diffusion throughout society
had come to seem outdated. Rousseau did not deny the
achievements of modern science, yet he maintained that there
were none the less grounds for mistrusting its moral value. In
doing so he gave new life to notions of 'virtue' that still
formed part of general moral language but whose connection
to current circumstances had become increasingly tenuous.
So tenuous, indeed, that Rousseau could invoke quite different meanings in the same text. What was virtue? A patri-
otic martial spirit or the conscientious fulfilment of universal
moral obligations? Blessed ignorance or merely the prudent
reservation of knowledge for those able to use it wisely? It
could be each or all of these. But the possible incompatibility
of these meanings mattered less than the fact that Rousseau
had managed to fuse different kinds of argument into an
overall indictment of things as they were. The categorical
condemnation of progress in the *Discourse on the Science
and the Arts* did not need to be taken at face value: by
legitimizing a general dissatisfaction it could be made to
serve a variety of specific purposes. In particular, it provided
ammunition in the ongoing debate over 'luxury', which
expressed, in various and often confusing combinations,
social anxieties about the erosion of traditional distinctions
of rank, moral or religious outrage at debauchery and waste;
and the claim advanced by thinkers of different stripes that
some degree of economic equality (at least among the pro-
pertied classes) was a necessary safeguard against political

corruption. Rousseau's 'outsider' rhetoric operated within a complex cultural framework in which many people who otherwise might have little in common with the author felt themselves marginalized too.

In the replies he made to critics of his first discourse, Rousseau became aware of the need to define his own intellectual position more carefully, but the broader issue of his rhetorical stance emerged more acutely in connection with other early works devoted to apparently less crucial matters. Rousseau's *Letter on French Music* (1753) provoked violent controversy because of its criticism of the French style of opera, which it compared unfavourably with the more 'natural' and passionate music of Italy. Readers might be forgiven for wondering why, if art distorted our understanding of virtue and distracted us from our duties, an austere moral censor should take such an enthusiastic part in an aesthetic quarrel, and even worse, offer an opera of his own (*The Village Soothsayer*, 1752) for public performance. In the preface to a play, *Narcissus*, that appeared the same year as the opera, Rousseau contended that his contradictions were those of the society itself in which he lived and to which he must speak. In a degraded world, art might provide emotional consolation or a saving image of virtue.

Obviously, this was not the whole truth. In both critical and expressive forms of language, Rousseau found resources of energy that overflowed the immediate, practical context. That vitality had a value of its own—but of what kind? While readers admired his rhetoric, critics were hard pressed to match its intensity with a clear intention. Rousseau was suspected of careerism and even of outright hypocrisy. There is no doubt he sought literary success, but the awkwardness and defensiveness of his self-justification point to a deeper problem. As in his critique of progress, Rousseau could not easily untangle himself from the discourses of his time. The first *Discourse* had succeeded because its indeterminacy allowed the public to read it in a variety of ways and the author to discover what he was trying to say through and against the language he had inherited. Aesthetic discourse is usually held to celebrate indeterminacy and tentative statement, but to his chagrin Rousseau initially found it more difficult to maintain his freedom of manœuvre in talking about art. The doctrine of imitation traditionally provided a way to mediate between artistic experiment and social responsibility. However, the narrow definition of imitation prevalent in classical French criticism proved too inflexible for Rousseau's purposes. In the *Letter on French Music* and his subsequent debate with the composer Jean-Philippe Rameau, Rousseau had to contend with what he felt was a reductive conception of musical art. He scorned the mechanical application of the rules of physics in Rameau's theory and the frozen lyrical conventions that passed for feeling in French opera. Similarly, when Rousseau published his novel *Julie* (1761), he would have to defend his heroine against those who insisted she was based on a real person and those who preferred to view her as the image of an intellectual ideal. Contemporary aesthetics could accommodate either view, but not Rousseau's conception of literary character as the locus of a felt but elusive psychological reality.

While these aesthetic quarrels may seem far removed from Rousseau's political concerns, the two domains are in fact linked. Rousseau pursued his discussion of music in the *Essay on the Origin of Languages*, which grew out of a footnote to the *Discourse on Inequality* but was published only in 1781, after the author's death. In the *Essay*, Rousseau connected the absence of real vigour and sentiment in song with the impossibility of attaining true political eloquence in any modern language. (Like many of his contemporaries, Rousseau was most concerned with vocal music, which he took to be the highest form of the art.) In eighteenth-century France, debates over language and artistic representation were not purely academic. Aesthetic controversies provided far more opportunity for creative discussion than any other social discourse, both in the range of subject-matter that could be included and in the freedom with which ideas could be connected and combined. They served as a testing-ground for beliefs and attitudes that would later help shape the political action that the paralysis of political discourse in the mid-eighteenth century seemed to defer. The *Discourse on Inequality*, which presents a hypothetical history of humanity based on an avowedly fictional state of nature, develops both from Rousseau's obligation to clarify his ideas about the relation between intellectual, moral, and social development, and from the controversy (which would soon give rise throughout Europe to debates about the sublime) about the kind of indeterminacy without which no freedom and expressive power can be sustained.

Like the first, this second *Discourse* was originally submitted in 1754 to the Dijon Academy, which had chosen inequality as the topic for its essay competition. In its advertisement, the Academy had asked, 'What is the source of inequality among men, and whether it is authorized by natural law.' In some respects, Rousseau's reply is less eccentric than his earlier submission. His was not the only entry to deny that natural law justified social inequality. Two others, including that of a former foreign minister, the marquis d'Argenson, did so as well. Even the winning essay by the abbé Talbert of Besançon took pains to distinguish the natural law that governed innocent humanity, under which all men were equal, from the one that came into force after the Fall of man and which alone justified inequality. Of course, this latter version of natural law was the only one with any practical significance, but Rousseau, too, would concede that a return to the state of nature as he defined it was impossible and that the workings of society made some inequality inevitable.

The *Discourse on Inequality* differs radically, however, from its competitors in tone and in scope. What makes it particularly fascinating is the way Rousseau stresses and stretches the meaning of its central term. With bitter eloquence he describes how inequalities of social esteem, of property, and of political power limit not only the individual's freedom to move and act as he pleases but his psychological balance as well (the French *inégal* can also refer to an 'uneven' temper). Rousseau declares that what may be inescapable is certainly intolerable. He seeks to persuade his readers that nothing could compensate them for this inner alienation. In Rousseau's text, inequality is not just a social fact; it conditions our very perception of the world.

In addition to emphasizing inequality as an inner experience, Rousseau vastly expands the range of external phenomena that need to be included in a proper analysis of the concept. Like other authors, he distinguishes between a natural inequality of physical strength or intellectual capacity and the kind of inequality that accompanies the growth of economic and political institutions. Like them, too, he traces the path that leads from one to the other, partly in historical terms by describing the way social life developed, partly by uncovering the structural logic of political rule. But in the contrast he draws between the independent man of the state of nature and the present condition of corrupted humanity, 'inequality' is more than a name for distinctions of wealth or power; it refers to any difference in material circumstances or in the perception of those circumstances that affects the way human beings live and understand themselves. Whether it be variations in the earth's climate or the comparisons people make between objects or between each other, the discovery—and the invention—of significant differences is the key to human development at every level.

Rousseau's radical approach to his topic may be seen most clearly in his discussion of the state of nature. This was a key concept in the natural rights theories of the seventeenth century. In the wake of the Reformation, which had broken down the religious unity of Europe, and of the rise of secular political states rationalizing the pursuit of national interests, these theories sought a new basis for law and morality, one that would accommodate a diversity of customs of beliefs (Tuck). Philosophical traditions inherited from Greece and Rome, or those too closely identified with a specific form of Christianity, were losing their universal validity as they came to be seen as expressions of a particular time or place. The religious and civil strife of the sixteenth century led many thinkers to become sceptical about the possibility of establishing a generally applicable, and generally persuasive, system of laws. The only solution seemed to lie in a disenchanted embrace of existing local customs, as in Montaigne, or in a hard-headed exploitation of political opportunity, as in Machiavelli.

Hugo Grotius, among other thinkers of the seventeenth century such as Hobbes and Samuel Pufendorf, saw a way to overcome scepticism without (as Pascal did) falling back into reliance on pure faith. Using as their point of departure the notion of a state of nature, that is, by subtracting from their description of humanity those elements associated with particular forms of civil association or codes of law, they hoped to gain agreement on a basis for defining any proper government, whatever its form. The principle they thought would command general assent was that a man had a natural right to preserve his life. This right, which no one in the state of nature would willingly give up, was not only to be acknowledged in civil society but also to be made the foundation of legitimate political obligation. The laws and procedures through which this fundamental right could be exercised were often (as in Hobbes) themselves called 'natural', but not because (as in classical or medieval natural law) they derived from an independent source of norms in nature itself. Rather, they were efficient rational means by which men could secure their lives. In the state of nature, survival was uncertain: the natural rights theorists appealed here to the sceptical awareness of human difference and unpredictability. The solution was to imagine men transferring to a central authority their natural right to decide for themselves how best to survive. Such a voluntary transfer thus provided a rationale for the power of the state, a foundation independent of religious beliefs or other traditions which, far from anchoring politics in a solid scheme of values, had become a source of dissension.

Natural rights theorists could and did disagree about the specifics of humanity's pre-political condition. Locke, who wished to limit the scope of political authority, described a 'state of nature' which encompassed family and economic relationships of a highly developed kind. The state served to guarantee their integrity rather than to foster their creation. Locke's outlook was less sceptical and, significantly, less persuasive for Rousseau than the more unsettling vision of

Hobbes. According to the latter, the state of nature was one in which men's unruly and unpredictable passions made survival a matter of competition and combat and prevented organized social development from occurring at all. Submission to the Hobbesian sovereign, precisely because it was absolute, provided a means for overcoming mutual suspicion. Pufendorf, a German jurist who believed in man's natural sociability and who exerted a strong influence throughout Protestant Europe (Rousseau had begun to read him while still a young man), downplayed the element of egotistical competition but emphasized the indigence of the state of nature, the lack of those moral and economic resources needed to develop men's distinctively human faculties. Those resources could only be mobilized through the creation of a stable framework of law.

Rousseau criticizes his predecessors for smuggling into their description of human life in the state of nature thoughts, passions, and conflicts that arose, in his opinion, only after society had begun to develop. The notion that the state of nature is one of material and moral poverty he also believes to result from an unwarranted projection of modern norms on to a situation quite unlike any with which we are familiar. In a way his criticism misses the point. The natural rights theorists were not defining a rigorously pure state of nature in and for itself. They were seeking a point of departure on which men of very different backgrounds could agree. However the state of nature was defined in detail, it was designed so that the transfer to a political authority of the rights enjoyed in it could be plausibly described and persuasively justified. It was, however, just this idea of a smooth transfer to which Rousseau objected. Grotius in particular he condemned, since the author of *The Laws of War and Peace* (1625), often honoured as the founder of modern international law, also included slavery among the legitimate transfers of natural right—natural rights being attributed to individuals precisely in order for their alienation to be imagined. If sheer survival is the primary consideration, then slavery is better than death. Not all natural rights theorists agreed with Grotius, but to varying degrees they shared the common strategy of depicting a state of independence in order to define acceptable forms of dependence. Rousseau, for whom personal independence was a priceless treasure, presents his state of nature with a very different purpose in mind. He wants to make it difficult for us to conceive how the transition from nature to civil (that is, political) society could have occurred. In doing so, he subjects the modern argument against scepticism to a sceptical critique, while at the same time his state of nature takes on a more ideal aspect.

Not that in Rousseau's state of nature life is any more prosperous or predictable than in Pufendorf or Hobbes. Men do not dominate nature in any way, for there is no stimulus to do so. Nor are there any grounds for knowing, trusting, or co-operating with each other. The difference is that it does not matter, for individuals live in isolation. Those who are healthy survive on what nature offers. Death comes quickly to the rest, and because they live entirely in the present they do not fear it. Human beings are independent of circumstances, not because their environment is stable, but because circumstances do not impinge on their consciousness. It is hard to imagine how this could be so, how, for example, a man could take no notice of changes in climate or a woman fail to recognize her own child. Rousseau is deliberately vague about where the state of nature might have existed and, in this first part of the *Discourse*, about the actual operation of human faculties. But Rousseau's point is primarily a negative one. In his view, as soon as men become aware of, say, the flood-cycle of the Nile, then they are no longer in the state of nature. For in responding to any difference of circumstance, even in the most elementary way and for their own survival, they are already embarked on the historical process that leads to social inequality. In disconnecting the state of nature from the unfolding of any kind of process other than the impersonal action of an undifferentiated nature, Rousseau provided a yardstick for measuring the contingency of all human relations.

Contemporary reactions to the *Discourse* focused almost exclusively on this portrait of the state of nature, which in some ways was even more disconcerting than that of Hobbes. *Leviathan*'s description of vainglory and struggle was harsh but dynamic. Rousseau is more benign, but the absence of dynamism scandalized enlightened critics. Voltaire's famous reply, in which he ironically announced a desire to walk on all fours after reading Rousseau, is typical in the way it neglects the nuances of the political polemic in order to focus on the image of man living in isolation, thinking only of the present, taking his food where he found it without reasoning (or worrying) about what would happen next. Of course, Rousseau accepts the fundamental role of self-preservation, and he does identify a principle of change in the idea of perfectibility. But he strips these ideas of their positive character. Self-preservation may be the basis of human action, but Rousseau, unlike Hobbes, does not immediately incorporate it into a system of value. The concept of perfectibility provides a key to human history, but it is not connected to a goal, either of biological adaptation or of moral perfection. Rousseau's state of nature thus extends the attack on corruption begun in the *Discourse on the Sciences and the Arts* without appealing to the other categories commonly used to frame such attacks. By describing perfect independence as a state in which man exercises no rule, appropriates no property, and exchanges nothing with others, Rousseau deprived discourses of civic virtue or sociable 'commerce' of their imaginative basis. Behind the mockery directed at the merely 'animal' character of Rousseau's state of nature was frustration at its resistance to discursive assimilation.

The marginal character of the *Discourse* may also explain why it provoked no official condemnation despite its disenchanted approach to political authority. The book was also published at a moment of political calm, just before the Seven Years War and the reaction against *philosophe* militancy in the late 1750s. Another factor is that, unlike the *Social Contract* and *Émile*, the *Discourse* avoided any direct attack on religion. Rousseau claimed that his portrait of the state of nature was a fiction that left aside the 'facts' of human origins as presented in the Bible. Such protests were common in philosophical works at the time, and the work could be tolerated as an exercise in pure speculation. But Rousseau's dismissal of fact had broader implications. More than a prudent gesture, it was an attempt to forestall the oppressive sense of closure to be found even in secular histories of mankind, including the rather pessimistic one he himself goes on to tell in the second part of the *Discourse*. The strategy succeeded, for as the century wore on and Voltaire's belief in the power of manners to stimulate improvement lost much of its appeal, Rousseau's state of nature offered an image of independence many readers found increasingly seductive.

This positive interpretation was supported by Rousseau's insistence on man's natural 'goodness'. In later years, especially in reaction to criticisms of his personal integrity, Rousseau would invest the term with a substantive ethical content, especially by linking goodness with the inner voice of conscience (not least his own). But in the *Discourse*, 'goodness' is used primarily to signal the absence of any specific moral character in human nature. Human will is fundamentally indeterminate. In any situation, men, unlike animals, may—for better or for worse—exceed or go against what nature requires. By using the term 'goodness', Rousseau distinguishes himself from the tradition that equated indeterminacy with corruption. The perfectibility of the human species is made possible by its lack of definition, and if Rousseau criticizes those who speak glibly of progress he also sets himself against the pessimistic tradition of French *moralistes* such as Pascal, for whom the restless mobility of desire is a sign of man's fallen nature. The other quality Rousseau attributes to man in the state of nature, the capacity for pity, also connects goodness with indeterminacy. In *Émile*, 'pity' is described as the source of benevolent concern for mankind, but in the *Discourse* it does not lead to close relationships with other people. (In the *Essay on the Origin of Languages* Rousseau will speak of love and tenderness, but the only real intimacy described in the *Discourse* will arise later, from the conflict of vanities.) Pity is essentially a reluctance to cause or witness suffering, and it can be called good just because it acts as a brake on aggression. Unlike other Enlightenment doctrines of compassion such as Adam Smith's, Rousseau's notion of pity serves primarily to guarantee that the drive for self-preservation is not harmful in its effects.

It is the unbounded character of human will, and man's freedom from circumstance generally, that makes the fictional state of nature something about which we should have 'accurate notions in order to judge our present state correctly'. Given Rousseau's sceptical critique of the natural rights theorists, to use the state of nature as a guide may seem contradictory. Nevertheless, after pointing out in the first part of the *Discourse* the difficulty of conceiving how human relationships ever arose, Rousseau takes pains to develop in the second part a logical, plausible account of the growth of social and political institutions. The chaos of the sixteenth century, against which Hobbes and others reacted so strongly, now seemed remote, and with a growing confidence in the ability of science to advance without overall metaphysical guarantees, a number of eighteenth-century writers found it possible to entertain the notion that, while necessary, an ideal standard is unreachable or uncertain and that analyses of particular phenomena may still possess broad explanatory power. This tendency can already be found in some French *moralistes*, whose disenchanted view of human nature led to acute psychological investigations increasingly divorced from direct connection with religion. In the early eighteenth century Bernard Mandeville gave the *moraliste* method a playful yet disturbing twist in his *Fable of the Bees*. Following the most rigorist of the French thinkers, he insisted that genuine virtue must be absolutely disinterested. He then demonstrated that most human action was not virtuous but then, by an ironic reversal, that what was usually called vice (the desire for luxury, for example) was in fact beneficial to humanity by stimulating industry and trade. In the *Discourse*, Rousseau attacked what he took to be Mandeville's cynical views, especially his paradoxical defence of inequality on utilitarian grounds, but in some ways his method resembles Mandeville's. Rousseau, too, will portray the ambivalent nature and paradoxical logic of each stage in human development.

Rousseau's peculiar combination of a renewed form of scepticism with explanatory confidence owes something to recent French thinkers as well. One of the most important is Buffon, an author whom Rousseau always held in the greatest respect and whose work is a major influence on the *Discourse*. Far from being a naïve and stolid empiricist, Buffon denied the possibility of certain knowledge of the external world (Roger). Scepticism informs his approach to the classification of species, as well as his hypotheses about the history of the universe. Yet, while his scepticism made him wary of humanity's pretensions to dominate the natural world, it did not lead to anxiety or a retreat from the investigation of nature. Rousseau disagreed with Buffon on a number of specific issues, but the scientist's example showed that instead of leading to a philosophical dead end, a sceptical attitude could open up new possibilities of interpretation. Rousseau's account of the invention of social and political institutions is often scathing, but it is energetically attentive to the interplay of chance, wilfulness, and material causes from which they emerge. A similar combination of scepticism and curiosity may be found in Montaigne, but in the eighteenth-century writers it has a broad anthropological as well as a psychological basis. It is notable, for example, that Rousseau agrees with Buffon that tool-making is not a cultural phenomenon so much as an extension of man's natural capacities. Despite Rousseau's insistence on the isolation of the individual consciousness in the state of nature, the transition to the use of objects and then to the (initially instrumental) contacts with other men in the second part of the text can be made with confidence—a confidence that extends to the exercise of Rousseau's own intellectual capacities.

The division of the *Discourse* into two uneven parts, the one descriptive and ideal, the other a narrative that recapitulates the first, inscribing its concepts in a real history, recalls the structure of two other influential works of the time. D'Alembert's *Preliminary Discourse* to the *Encyclopaedia* (1751) first offers a synoptic view of the forms of knowledge and then a history of their discovery and rediscovery in the Renaissance. Condillac's *Essay on the Origin of Human*

Knowledge (1746) begins with an analysis of the 'materials' of knowledge, rising in an orderly way from sensation to the 'operations of the soul' and then to the signs we give to our ideas; the second part of the book spirals back to the historical origin of signs and traces the somewhat less orderly story of how language evolved from metaphorical speech, hieroglyphs, and song to the more methodical style of modern philosophy. In neither work does the hypothetical logical order and the actual order of discovery coincide. From a practical point of view the first part of each book might have been dropped entirely, but while there are important discrepancies between the two parts, the authors hold on to both. Wanting to avoid the twin pitfalls of metaphysical abstraction and a historical scheme deprived of broader philosophical value, they keep their options open. This produces another kind of destabilizing 'inequality', this time in the form of the text itself.

The dynamic of history in the second part of the *Discourse* is itself propelled by a curious mixture of material necessity and rhetorical mystification. Rousseau begins by imagining property as emerging when a man claimed a field as his own and found others naïve enough to believe him, but the arbitrariness of the gesture is counterbalanced by a sophisticated analysis of different modes of production and of the successive stages of human organization, from hunting and gathering to pastoral (discussed in more detail in the *Essay on the Origin of Languages*) to settled agricultural society. This aspect of Rousseau's analysis connects the *Discourse* to the most advanced trends in eighteenth-century social science (Meek).

Equally important for understanding the emergence of political institutions, however, is the way language develops. In a fragment of an early version of the *Discourse*, Rousseau discusses how in primitive societies such as ancient Egypt, where knowledge of writing was confined to a priestly élite, linguistic mastery was closely linked with mystification and oppression of the people. The idea was a staple of the anticlerical circle around d'Holbach. But while Rousseau includes vivid images of wilfulness such as the 'inventor' of property, the *Discourse* dissociates language from personal intention. Instead, language becomes a structuring principle in its own right. In the first part of the text, Rousseau argued against Condillac that it is hard to imagine how even the simplest words came into use. Because men in the pure state of nature would not have noticed the similarities and differences among objects, they would hardly be able to create a common noun such as 'tree'. When they do begin to notice such things, it is still difficult to imagine how a stable language could emerge, for 'the first idea we derive from two things is that they are not the same'. Only later, at a more sophisticated stage, will men be able to ignore those differences and designate a number of different objects by the one word 'tree'. As Paul de Man has shown, the development of language and its conceptual categories prefigures the process by which inequality is perceived, institutionalized, and covered over in political society where rich and poor band together to provide 'equal' protection to all. For the first social contract to take place, obvious disparities of wealth must be overlooked. Otherwise the poor would never have agreed to it. One could speak of a conjuror's trick, but, on Rousseau's terms, any subsequent demand for 'real' equality is also based on a conceptual fiction, since it must overlook differences in men's strength or talent. The evolution of political forms in the *Discourse*, from the time when people first sought respect and consideration from others through the formulation of the first laws to the collapse of law into despotism, involves a complicated play of linguistic comparisons, generalizations, and unstable metaphors.

A similar process occurs in Rousseau's own narrative, which uses terms such as 'natural' or 'legitimate' to describe forms of behaviour or social organization whose origin he has unmasked as violent or artificial. Like all other moments in the progress of human society, such forgetting also has its advantages, for how else could any community be formed, and how else could we communicate persuasively? Rousseau's account of inequality is thus much more subtle and double-edged than his treatment of corruption in the *Discourse on the Sciences and the Arts*. Clearly, Rousseau wants us to be more sceptically conscious about the process by which the integrity of individual objects, and of individual persons, is subsumed under more general concepts. Yet, the pessimistic conclusion of the *Discourse* seems to offer few grounds for believing that raising the reader's consciousness will lead to a happy solution. Rousseau's account of political life leads to a despotic nightmare in which all men are once again equal because they are all nothing. Although he envisions the possibility of 'revolutions' that might bring governments closer to their earlier and more legitimate form, he does not say how this could happen, or, indeed, whether such a revolution would not repeat the basic pattern of history. An actual return to the state of nature is, of course, impossible. Neither is it clear how the idea of the state of nature, vital as it is to reopening an imaginative space of indeterminacy, could offer a guide to better judgement. On the contrary, if the meaning of such key terms as 'man' emerges from a combination of error and forgetting in an impersonal process that coincides with humanity's mental and moral development as a whole, then the very possibility of transcending that process is undermined. A similar question might also be raised about the author's own role as a guide. Determining Rousseau's own position and the ultimate thrust of his argument is no less problematic in the *Discourse on Inequality* than it was in Rousseau's earlier works.

Rousseau does attempt to 'place' himself with respect to his argument by dedicating his work to the Republic of Geneva. In the epistle dedicatory, he also offers a redeeming image of a society able to strike a successful balance between equality and inequality, between freedom and order. Rousseau had been readmitted to citizenship in 1754, shortly after submitting the first version of the *Discourse* to the Dijon Academy, and in the published text he not only describes himself as a citizen of Geneva on the title-page, he places an engraving of the republic's coat of arms at the beginning of his dedication. The confident motto under the city's coat of arms—*Post tenebras lux* ('After the darkness, light')—belies Rousseau's equation of progress with decline. Rousseau goes on to extol the republic's constitution, praising the wisdom with which natural equality and social inequality have been combined to reconcile public order and private happiness. So hyperbolic are the terms of the epistle that one wonders whether Rousseau was deluding himself or being ironic. Certainly he glosses over the tensions between the oligarchy that actually governed the city and the body of the citizens, whose political power was only nominal. Rousseau had not seen Geneva for many years when he composed his dedication, and so it is not surprising, especially given his increasing disenchantment with life in Paris, that he should be tempted to idealize his native land.

The political tensions that had periodically arisen in Geneva since the beginning of the eighteenth century, when a number of citizens had begun to chafe under the republic's oligarchical rule, are none the less indirectly acknowledged in Rousseau's letter. In dedicating his book to the republic— that is, to the citizens, whom he addresses by their formal title of 'Sovereign Lords'—and not to the governing council, Rousseau undercuts the tribute he pays to the 'magistrates' by alluding to the derivative character of their power. On the other hand, he does not say the citizens should recover any political initiative. Does he mean to suggest it? Or does the dedication simply offer an image of moral energy framed by a political order it invigorates but does not change? In the latter case, the portrait of the Genevan citizenry would parallel the description of the state of nature. In both cases, we see a free will operating independently of circumstance— an appealing image Rousseau does not believe is spoiled by the objection that this will has no practical effect. On the contrary, given the *Discourse*'s analysis of historical cause and effect as links in an oppressive chain of events, this lack of determination only adds to that image's charm—for the author no less than for the reader.

Rousseau's description of Geneva may or may not have been intended to be fictional, like the portrait of the state of nature. Whatever the case, in its peculiar dynamic of energy without specific practical purpose, and in its imaginative appeal to a spectator who is at once absorbed by it and yet detached, it may be termed aesthetic in character, for these are the very categories in which eighteenth-century writers try to account for the power of art. Although Rousseau is generally critical of the aesthetic discourse of his time, in his *Letter to d'Alembert* (1758) he will pursue an aesthetic kind of politics in proposing the institution of public festivals as an alternative to the theatre. Four years later the *Social Contract*, too, would add to the logic of the general will a structure of mutual identification and helpful belief as an essential support for political freedom.

But if the progress of civilization is so alienating and in the end so destructive of liberty, how could Rousseau's redemptive images have any effect at all? Geneva's achievement of republican freedom in the face of French political and cultural power indicates that there are exceptions to the general pattern of decline, but how did Geneva escape the levelling process that reduces all citizens to slaves? Rousseau does not explain, but we gain some insight into what he is doing if we compare his history of society with the histories of political economy written about the same time in another small country, one that, like Geneva, shared a language and a border with a powerful and sophisticated neighbour. Writing in the *Edinburgh Review*, Adam Smith was impressed with Rousseau's rhetoric, but he thought the author rescued his idealism only through 'a little philosophical chemistry', i.e. alchemy. Adam Ferguson, who shared many of Rousseau's worries about the corruption of virtue in modern society, also thought the *Discourse* misguided. In his *Essay on the History of Civil Society* (1767), he pointed out that the free European republics existed only on sufferance: neighbouring monarchies could easily crush them if they wished. The point had already been made by Hobbes, but it took on new meaning for Scottish intellectuals considering the implications for their country's improvement of its union with England in 1707. It was the Scottish political economists who offered the most comprehensive theory of the different modes of production that mark the stages in humanity's progress. More than the three stages discussed by Rousseau, they were interested by the fourth stage, that of commercial society, for they believed it contained the promise of real freedom, personal and social if not specifically political in nature. This freedom was not viewed as purely egotistical, for a genuine refinement of manners, even a new form of virtue, would emerge from relationships in which rank and other considerations of fixed status were superseded by more open and flexible forms of sociability—'commerce' as discursive interaction as well as trade.

Rousseau attacked this doctrine as a cruel hoax which only perpetuated the oppression of the poor and imprisoned the rest in stifling rituals of social conformity. Commercial politeness was for him as much of a mystification as the beneficial exchange of rights for security advocated by Hobbes and Grotius. Significantly, Rousseau does not describe the shift from a traditional agricultural society to a dynamic commercial one. Indeed, in the last moments of Rousseau's history politics displaces production altogether. While Rousseau attacks luxury and other manifestations of civilization in a general way, his analysis of despotism is not based on a material mode of production as such but on a debasement of language connected with a deep psychological alienation that mere economic initiative cannot undo. Rousseau thus offers a powerful critique of his more optimistic contemporaries' hopes. But one might argue that it is precisely this emphasis on the political as an ultimate and distinct stage of development that allows Rousseau himself to imagine a reversal of the sad situation described at the end of the *Discourse*. To the extent that politics, like the state of nature, is not tied to actual circumstances, freedom might be recovered through a pure act of will revitalizing the metaphors that constitute political identity.

Rousseau will pursue his attempt to reconceive the political realm as the true locus of freedom in the *Social Contract*. But his association of the political with the transcendence of specific action raises questions about the emancipatory potential of aesthetic forms just as serious as those provoked by the refinement of manners through commerce. One is the connection between these forms and the practical underpinnings of autonomy. Rousseau omits economic considerations from his description of Geneva. Because of its need for gold, Geneva's watchmaking trade was relatively capital-intensive: the free artisan-citizens with whom Rousseau identifies were linked to a complex economic network. The city was also an important financial clearing-house, and if France found it convenient to support Genevan independence, it was partly to preserve a useful 'offshore' centre of credit. Ferguson's point about the independence of republics was well taken: one cannot forget the circumstances that make independence possible.

An even thornier problem emerges, however, when Rousseau does imagine his vision in practice. In the *Discourse*, history is an impersonal process. Similarly, in appropriating aesthetic categories as a way to escape that process, Rousseau also insists on the separation of art from the artist as essential to the productive indeterminacy of will and imagination. But the problematic role of the Legislator in the *Social Contract* and the tutor in *Émile*, educating and edifying the citizen by orchestrating seductive images of happiness compromises that distinction. The artist's freedom becomes the audience's constraint. Rousseau's writings offer a vivid example of the pitfalls as well as the possibilities of endowing aesthetic freedom with political form.

NOTE ON THE TEXT

THE *Discourse on Inequality* was first published in 1755, with a second edition incorporating corrections and minor changes appearing the same year. In the posthumous edition of 1782 there are further changes and additions. A recently rediscovered copy of the first edition with corrections in Rousseau's hand confirms the authenticity of many of these changes. For textual details, readers should refer to the critical editions by Jean Starobinski (the 1992 separate printing of the *Discourse* offers a revised version of his edition in the complete works, along with a detailed commentary) and, for an exhaustive study of variants, by Heinrich Meier. This translation is based on the editions of 1755 and includes the most important additions of the 1782 edition. The bibliography of critical works on Rousseau is limited to works available in English along with a very few of the most important French-language studies.

SELECT BIBLIOGRAPHY

Editions of Rousseau

Œuvres complètes, ed. Bernard Gagnebin and Marcel Raymond (Paris, 1959–   ).

Discours sur l'origine et les fondements de l'inégalité parmi les hommes, ed. Jean Starobinski (Paris, 1985, 1992).

Diskurs über die Ungleichheit/Discours sur l'inégalité, ed. Heinrich Meier, 2nd edn. (Paderborn, 1990).

Biography

Maurice Cranston, Jean-Jacques: The Life and Work of Jean-Jacques Rousseau 1712–1754 (London, 1982); The Noble Savage: Jean-Jacques Rousseau 1754–1762 (London, 1991). A third volume is forthcoming.

Critical Works

Keith Michael Baker, Inventing the French Revolution (Cambridge, 1990).

Howard R. Cell and James I. MacAdam, Rousseau's Response to Hobbes (New York, 1988).

John Charvet, The Social Problem in the Philosophy of Rousseau (Cambridge, 1974).

Patrick Coleman, Rousseau's Political Imagination (Geneva, 1984).

Robert Derathé, Rousseau et la science politique de son temps (Paris, 1950).

Jacques Derrida, Of Grammatology, trans. G. Spivak (Baltimore, 1976).

Peter France, Politeness and its Discontents (Cambridge, 1992).

Victor Goldschmidt, Anthropologie et politique: Les principes du système de Rousseau (Paris, 1974).

Victor Gourevitch, 'Rousseau's Pure State of Nature', Interpretation, 16 (1988–9), 23–59.

J. C. Hall, Rousseau (London, 1973).

George R. Havens, Voltaire's Marginalia on the Pages of Rousseau (Columbus, 1933).

Nannerl O. Keohane, Philosophy and the State in France (Princeton, NJ, 1980).

Claude Lévi-Strauss, *Totemism*, trans. R. Needham (Boston, 1963).

Paul de Man, *Allegories of Reading* (New Haven, Conn., 1979).

Roger Masters, *The Political Philosophy of Rousseau* (Princeton, NJ, 1968).

Ronald L. Meek, *Social Science and the Ignoble Savage* (Cambridge, 1976).

Susan Moller Okin, *Women in Western Political Thought* (Princeton, NJ, 1979).

Anthony Pagden (ed.), *The Languages of Political Theory in Early Modern Europe* (Cambridge, 1987).

J. G. A. Pocock, *Virtue, Commerce, and History* (Cambridge, 1985).

Jacques Roger, *Buffon* (Paris, 1989).

Judith N. Shklar, *Men and Citizens: A Study of Rousseau's Theory* (Cambridge, 1969).

Jean Starobinski, *Jean-Jacques Rousseau: Transparency and Obstruction*, trans. A. Goldhammer (Chicago, 1988).

Susan Staves and John Brewer (eds.), *Property and Political Theory* (New York, forthcoming).

Richard Tuck, *Natural Rights Theories* (Cambridge, 1979).

Robert Wokler, *Rousseau on Society, Politics, Music and Language: An Historical Interpretation of His Early Writings* (New York, 1987).

—— *Rousseau* (Oxford, forthcoming).

A CHRONOLOGY OF
JEAN-JACQUES ROUSSEAU

1712	Rousseau is born in Geneva.
1722	After his father's departure for Nyon, he and his cousin live with pastor Lambercier, a family friend.
1725	Rousseau is apprenticed to Abel Du Commun, a master engraver.
1728	Finding himself locked out of the city one night, Rousseau decides to leave Geneva. In Annecy, he meets Mme de Warens for the first time and is sent to Turin, where he converts to Catholicism and enters the service of the comte de Gouvon.
1729	Dismissed from his position, Rousseau returns to Mme de Warens, where he stays, despite intermittent periods of wandering in France and Switzerland.
1740	Rousseau enters the Mably household in Lyons as tutor.
1742	Arrives in Paris, hoping to make his fortune with a new system of musical notation.
1743	Leaves for Venice as secretary to the French ambassador.
1744	Resigns his position and returns to Paris.
1745	Meets Thérèse Levasseur, who becomes his companion, and is in touch with Diderot and Condillac.
1746	Rousseau becomes secretary to Mme Dupin, wife of the wealthy tax-collector Claude Dupin, and her stepson Dupin de Francueil.
1749	Writes articles on music for the *Encyclopaedia*. After sudden 'illumination' on the way to visit Diderot in prison, composes *Discourse on the Sciences and the Arts*, which is published a year later.
1752	Rousseau's opera, *The Village Soothsayer*, successfully produced at Fontainebleau.
1753	Publishes *Letter on French Music* and begins *Discourse on Inequality*.
1754	Visits Geneva for the first time since 1737, returns to Calvinist Church, and is readmitted to citizenship.
1755	Publishes *Discourse on Inequality*.
1756	Rousseau leaves Paris for the country, settling in a cottage

on Mme d'Épinay's estate. He begins a novel to be titled *Julie, or the New Héloïse*.

1758 Publishes *Letter to d'Alembert on Stage-performances*, breaks with Diderot.

1759 Rousseau moves to Montmorency, near the home of the maréchal de Luxembourg.

1761 Publishes *Julie*, which becomes a best seller.

1762 Publishes the *Social Contract* and *Émile*. Both are condemned in Geneva. In France, the *Social Contract* is banned, and *Émile*, a treatise on education containing a profession of faith in a natural religion, is condemned. A warrant is issued for Rousseau's arrest and he flees to Switzerland.

1763 Publishes *Letter to Christophe de Beaumont*, archbishop of Paris, to defend *Émile*.

1764 Publishes *Letters from the Mountain* in reply to political and religious attacks from Geneva.

1765 Driven from his home in Neuchâtel, Rousseau begins a nomadic life. Short period of intense happiness on the island of Saint-Pierre in the lake of Bienne.

1766 Arrives in England, writes *Confessions*, quarrels with Hume.

1767 Returns to France, living in various provincial towns under an assumed name, continues to write *Confessions*.

1770 Rousseau is allowed to return to Paris. He composes several books, including *Considerations on the Government of Poland*, *Rousseau Judge of Jean-Jacques*, but publishes nothing in the remaining years of his life.

1776 Begins his final work, the *Reveries of the Solitary Walker*.

1778 Shortly after moving to Ermenonville at the invitation of the marquis de Girardin, Rousseau dies.

1782–9 Rousseau's autobiographical works are published posthumously. His late political writings will only be fully published in the nineteenth century.

1794 Rousseau's ashes are transferred to the Panthéon.

DISCOURSE ON THE ORIGIN AND FOUNDATIONS OF INEQUALITY AMONG MEN

by

JEAN-JACQUES ROUSSEAU
citizen of Geneva

We must seek what is natural not in perverted beings,
but in those who act in accordance with nature.
Aristotle, *Politics*, I. 5. 1254[a].

TO THE REPUBLIC OF GENEVA
Magnificent, Most Honoured, and Sovereign Lords:*

CONVINCED that only the virtuous citizen is entitled to offer his homeland the honours it can acknowledge, I have laboured for thirty years to earn the right to offer you public homage. Because this happy occasion partly compensates for what my efforts have failed to do, I thought it admissible here to heed more the zeal that stirs me than the right that should be my justification. Having had the good fortune to be born among you, how could I reflect on the equality that nature has placed in men and the inequality they themselves have instituted, without reflecting on the deep wisdom with which both, felicitously combined in this city-state, work together, in a fashion closest to natural law and most favourable for society, toward the preservation of public order and the well-being of individuals? In searching for the best maxims that good sense can dictate concerning the constitution of a government, I have been so impressed at seeing them all enacted in yours that even had I not been born within your walls, I would have been compelled to offer this picture of human society to the one people that, among all others, appears to possess the greatest advantages of society and to have best forestalled its abuses.

If I could have chosen my birthplace, I would have chosen a society of a size limited by the range of the human faculties, that is to say, by the possibility of being well governed, and one in which, since everyone is equal to his tasks, no one would be compelled to entrust his responsibilities to others; a state in which all individuals were acquainted with each other, and neither the shady schemes of vice nor the modesty of virtue could escape public view and public judgement; and in which the agreeable habit of seeing and knowing one another would make the love of one's country take the form of love of its citizens rather than of its soil.

I would have wished to be born in a country where the sovereign and the people could have one and the same interest only, so that the movement of the civil mechanism conduced only to the common happiness. Since this is impossible unless the people and the sovereign are one and the same being, it follows that I would have wished to be born under a wisely tempered democratic government.

I would have wished to live and die free, that is to say, so thoroughly subject to the laws that neither I nor anyone else could shake off their honorable yoke—that light and salutary yoke that the proudest heads bear with all the more docility as they are made to bear no other.

Thus, I would have wished that no one in the state could claim he was above the law, and that no one from outside the state could dictate a law that the state was obliged to recognize. For regardless of how a government is formally constituted, if there is a single man not subject to the law, all the others are necessarily at that man's mercy. (A) And if there is a national ruler, and a foreign ruler as well, no matter how they divide up their authority, it is impossible for both leaders to be duly obeyed and the state well governed.

I would not have wished to live in a newly created republic, regardless of how good its laws were, for fear that the government might not fit the exigencies of the moment, either by not suiting the new citizens or they it, so that the state would be liable to upheavals and disintegration almost from birth. For freedom is like those heavy and succulent foods or full-bodied wines that can sustain and fortify the robust constitutions that are used to them, but that overcome, ruin, and intoxicate the weak and delicate ones that are unused to them. Once accustomed to masters, people become incapable of doing without them. When they try to shake off the yoke, they move still further from freedom, taking it for an unbridled licence that is in fact its very opposite, and their revolutions almost always deliver them into the hands of seducers who then bind their chains ever tighter. Even the Roman people, that model for all free peoples, were unable to govern themselves when they first emerged from the oppression of the Tarquins. Degraded by the slavery and ignominious work imposed on them, the Romans were at first merely a witless herd who had to be treated with care and governed with the utmost wisdom to allow time for them gradually to grow accustomed to breathing the wholesome air of freedom. Those souls, enervated or rather brutalized under tyranny, by degrees acquired the austere morals and noble courage that eventually made the Romans the most admirable of all peoples. I would have thus sought for my country a happy and quiet republic whose age was lost, as it were, in the mists of time;* a republic that underwent only such stresses as might bring forth and bolster its inhabitants' courage and love of country, and one in which the citizens, long used to wise independence, were not just free but worthy of freedom.

I would have chosen a country, diverted from the fierce lust for conquest by a fortunate lack of power, and protected by an even more fortunate location from the fear of itself becoming the object of conquest by any other state: a free nation situated among several different nations, none with any interest in invading it and each with an interest in preventing others from invading it—in short, a republic that did not tempt the ambitions of its neighbours and that could reasonably count on their help in case of need. It follows that in such a fortunate situation it would have nothing to fear but itself, and if its citizens were trained in arms, it would be more for the sake of maintaining that soldierly spirit and noble courage that are so well suited to freedom and cultivate the taste for it rather than from the necessity for the citizens' actual defence.

I would have sought out a country where the right of legislation was common to all citizens—for who better than they can know under what conditions it suits them to live together in one society? But I would not favour plebiscites like those of the Romans in which the leaders of state and those with the greatest stake in its preservation were excluded from the deliberations on which its security often depended and in which, by an absurd illogic, the magistrates were deprived of the rights enjoyed by ordinary citizens.

On the contrary, I would have wished that, as a means of

checking self-seeking, ill-conceived projects and dangerous innovations like those that finally drove the Athenians to defeat, no one should have the power to propose new laws according to his fancy; that this right be vested uniquely in the magistrates, and that they would invoke this right so circumspectly that the people would be so guarded in consenting to these laws, and that the laws could be promulgated only with such solemnity that, before that constitution could be disturbed, everyone would have time to realize that it is primarily the great antiquity of laws that makes them sacred and venerable, and that the people soon learn contempt for laws they see changed every day; that in becoming accustomed to disregarding ancient usages in the name of improvement, great evils are often introduced to correct lesser ones.

I would above all have fled a republic, as necessarily ill-governed, in which the people, thinking they could do without magistrates or allow them only a precarious authority, would have foolishly reserved for themselves the administration of civil affairs and the execution of their own laws. This must have been the primitive constitution of the first governments just after emerging from the state of nature, and this too was one of the failings that proved the downfall of the republic of Athens.

But I would have chosen a republic in which individuals, content with approving the laws and making collective decisions on proposals from the leaders about the most important public business, had established respected courts, carefully distinguished the jurisdiction of each one, and annually elected the most capable and upright of their fellow citizens to administer justice and govern the state. In such a republic, the virtue of the magistrates would give such clear evidence of the wisdom of the people that each would do the other reciprocal honour, so that if ever tragic misunderstandings disturbed the civil harmony, even the intervals of blindness and error would be marked by intimations of moderateness, mutual esteem, and a shared respect for the laws—harbingers and guarantees of a sincere and lasting reconciliation.

Such, Magnificent, Most Honoured, and Sovereign Lords, are the advantages I would have sought in the homeland I chose. And if providence had added a charming location, a temperate climate, fertile soil, and the most delightful vistas under the sun, to complete my happiness I would have wished only to enjoy all these blessings in the bosom of that fortunate country, living peaceably in sweet society with my fellow citizens, practising toward them, following their example, humanity, friendship, and all the virtues, and leaving after me the honourable memory of a good man, an upright and virtuous patriot.

If, less fortunate or wise too late, I were reduced to ending an infirm and indolent life in other climes, vainly regretting the repose and peace of which a misspent youth had robbed me, I would have at least kept alive in my soul the feelings that I was unable to express in my own country, and filled with a tender and disinterested love for my distant fellow citizens, I would have addressed them from the depths of my heart some such words as these:

'My dear fellow citizens, or rather my brothers, because nearly all of us are united by the ties of blood as well as those of law, it pleases me that I cannot think of you without immediately recalling all the blessings you enjoy and whose value perhaps none of you appreciates more than do I who have lost them. The more I reflect on your political and civil arrangements, the less I can imagine that the nature of human affairs could produce a better one. In all other governments, when there is a question of securing the greatest good of the state, nothing ever goes beyond hypothetical projects and at most mere possibilities. As for you, your happiness is already a reality, you have only to enjoy it, and to become perfectly happy, you need only be able to content yourselves with being so. Your sovereignty, acquired or recovered at the point of a sword and preserved for two centuries through valour and wisdom, is at last fully and universally recognized.* Honourable treaties fix your borders, secure your rights, and assure your tranquillity. Your constitution is excellent, dictated by the most sublime reason and protected by friendly and estimable powers. Your state is peaceful; you have neither wars nor conquerors to fear. Your only masters are the wise laws initiated by yourselves and administered by the upright magistrates you have chosen. You are neither rich enough to become weakened through indolence and to lose in vain delights the taste for true happiness and sturdy virtue, nor poor enough to need more external assistance than your own industry can procure. And the precious freedom that in the great nations is maintained only through exorbitant taxes, costs you almost nothing to preserve.

'May a republic so wisely and fortunately constituted last for ever, both for the well-being of its citizens and as an example to other peoples. This is the only wish left for you to make, and the only precaution left for you to take. It now depends on you, not to create your happiness, for your ancestors have spared you that effort, but to make your happiness endure by using it wisely and well. Your preservation depends on your perpetual union, your obedience to the law, and your respect for its administrators. If there remains among you one grain of bitterness and mistrust, promptly destroy it as a baneful leaven that would sooner or later result in your misfortune and the ruin of the state. I entreat you all to look into the depths of your hearts and heed the secret voice of conscience. Does any among you know anywhere in the world a body more upright, enlightened, and estimable than that of your magistracy? Do not all of its members set an example of moderation, simplicity of morals, respect for the laws, and the most sincere spirit of reconciliation? Then freely and unreservedly give those wise leaders the salutary confidence that reason owes to virtue; bear in mind that it is you who have chosen them, that they have justified your choice, and that the honours owed to those whom you have set in high positions necessarily reflect on yourselves. None of you is so unenlightened as to be ignorant that when the force of the laws and the authority of their defenders are weakened, there can be neither security nor freedom for anyone. What then is at issue among you other than doing wholeheartedly and with justified confidence what you would in any case be obliged to do out of enlightened self-interest, duty, and reason? May a culpable and fatal indifference to the defence of the constitution never cause you to neglect, in time of need, the wise counsel of the most enlightened and zealous of your fellow citizens, but may equity, moderation, and the most respectful firmness of purpose continue to regulate all your actions and to display you to the whole world as an example of a valiant and modest people, as jealous of its glory as of its freedom. Beware above all—and this will be my last piece of advice to you—of listening to sinister interpretations and malicious rumours, the secret motives of which are often more dangerous that the actions they report. A whole household is awakened and takes warning at the first cry of a good and faithful watchdog who never barks except at the approach of burglars. But people hate the nuisance caused by those noisy animals that continually disturb the public peace and whose incessant, ill-timed warnings are not heeded even when they are called for.'

And you, Magnificent and Most Honoured Lords, you worthy and revered magistrates of a free people, permit me to offer you in particular my homage and my respect. If the world holds a rank suitable for conferring glory on those who occupy it, it is surely the one acquired by talents and virtue, the rank of which you have proved yourselves worthy and to which your fellow citizens have raised you. Their own merit adds to yours a new lustre, and I find that you, who were elected by men capable of governing others in order to govern themselves, are placed as far above other magistrates as a free people—and particularly the free people whom you have the honour of leading—is, through its enlightenment and reason, above the peoples of other states.

May I be permitted to cite an example of which better records ought to have been preserved and which will always be near to my heart? I never recall without the most tender emotions the memory of the virtuous citizen* to whom I owe my birth and who often spoke to me in childhood of the respect that is due you. I see him living still by the work of his hands and nourishing his soul with the most sublime truths. I see Tacitus, Plutarch, and Grotius intermixed with the tools of his trade in front of him. I see at his side a beloved son receiving with too little profit the gentle instruction of the best of fathers. But if the follies of a misspent youth made me forget those wise lessons for a time, I had the good fortune at last to realize that whatever one's inclinations to vice, an education that has engaged the heart is unlikely to be lost forever.

Such, Magnificent and Most Honoured Lords, are the citizens—and even the simple inhabitants*—born in the state you govern. Such are those educated and sensible men of whom such base and false ideas are entertained in other countries, where they are spoken of as 'the workers' or 'the people'. My father, I gladly admit, was in no way prominent among his fellow citizens. He was merely what they all are and yet he was such that nowhere was his company not sought after, cultivated, and profitably too, by the most upright men. It is not fitting for me—nor, thank heaven, is it necessary for anyone else—to speak to you of the regard that you can expect from men of that stamp, your equals in both education and the rights of nature and birth, your inferiors by their own will and by the preference that they owe—and grant—your merit, a preference for which you in turn owe them a species of gratitude. I learn with keen satisfaction how much gentleness and fellow feeling you temper, in your dealings with them, the gravity suited to the ministers of the law; how much you repay them in esteem and thoughtful attention for what they owe you in obedience and respect, conduct so full of justice and wisdom that it serves to take ever further from living memory the unfortunate events* that must be forgotten if they are never to be seen again, conduct all the more judicious because this equitable and generous people makes its duty a pleasure and naturally loves to honour you, and those most zealous in upholding their own rights are the ones most inclined to respect yours.

It ought not to be surprising that the leaders of a civil society should love its glory and happiness, but, unfortunately for men's tranquillity, it is surprising when those who regard themselves as magistrates, or rather the masters of a holier and more sublime homeland, exhibit any love for the earthly country that nourishes them. How pleasing it is to be able to make such a rare exception in our favour, and to number among the ranks of our best citizens those zealous custodians of the sacred articles established by the laws, those venerable shepherds of souls, whose lively and sweet eloquence all the better instils the maxims of the Gospel in men's hearts because they themselves always begin by practising what they preach! Everyone knows with what success the great art of preaching is cultivated in Geneva. But since people are all too accustomed to observing things said in one way and done in another, few realize just how much the spirit of Christianity, the sanctity of morals, and discipline of oneself and gentleness toward others prevail in our clergy. Perhaps only the city of Geneva can offer the edifying example of such a perfect union between a society of theologians and men of letters. I base my hope for its tranquillity largely on their acknowledged wisdom, moderation, and zeal for the prosperity of the state. I note, with pleasure and surprise and respect, the clergy's abhorrence of the frightful maxims of those holy and barbarous men, of whom history provides more than one example, who, to uphold the alleged rights of God—that is to say, their own interests—have been all the less sparing of human blood because they flattered themselves that their own would always be respected.

Could I forget that precious half of the republic that assures the happiness of the other and whose sweetness and goodness maintain its peace and good morals? Amiable and virtuous women of Geneva, the destiny of your sex will always be to govern our destiny.* Happy are we when your chaste power, exercised solely within the marriage bond, makes itself felt only for the glory of the state and the well-being of the public. Thus it is that in Sparta the women were in command, and thus it is that you deserve to be in command in Geneva. What barbarous man could resist the voice of honour and reason in the mouth of a gentle wife? And who would not despise vain luxury on seeing your simple and modest garb that, getting its lustre from the wearer, seems all the more becoming to beauty? It is for you, by your amiable and innocent dominion and by your subtle wit, always to uphold the love of laws within the state and concord among the citizens, to reunite by happy marriages families that are divided, and, above all, to correct, through the persuasive sweetness of your lessons and the modest graces of your conversation, the excesses that our young people pick up in other countries, from which, instead of the many useful things that might profit them, they bring back, with childish manners and ridiculous airs acquired from loose women, an admiration of who knows what kinds of so-called grandeurs, those frivolous compensations for servitude that would never match the true value of august freedom. Therefore, always remain as you are, the chaste guardians of our morals and all the gentle bonds of peace, asserting on every occasion the rights of the heart and of nature in the interest of duty and virtue.

I flatter myself that events will not prove me wrong in basing on such guarantees my hopes for the general happiness of the citizens and of the glory of the republic. I admit that with all these advantages, the republic will not shine with the brilliance that dazzles most eyes, the childish and fatal taste for which is the most mortal enemy of happiness and freedom. Let a dissolute youth search elsewhere for easy pleasures and long repentance. Let so-called people of taste admire in other places the grandeur of palaces, the beauty of carriages, the sumptuous furnishings, the pomp of ceremonies, and all the refinements of softness and luxury. In Geneva, we find only men, but such a spectacle has a value of its own and those who appreciate it are worth more than the admirers of all the rest.

May you all, Magnificent, Most Honoured and Sovereign Lords, deign to accept with the same goodness my respectful assurances of the interest I take in your common prosperity. If I have been so unlucky as to be guilty of some rash enthusiasm in this lively effusion from the heart, I beg you to forgive it as due to the tender affection of a true patriot and the ardent and legitimate zeal of a man who imagines no greater happiness for himself than that of seeing you all happy.

I am, with the most profound respect, Magnificent, Most

Honoured, and Sovereign Lords, your humble and most obedient servant and fellow citizen,

JEAN-JACQUES ROUSSEAU

Chambéry, 12 June 1754

PREFACE

OF all the areas of human knowledge, the most valuable but least advanced seems to be that of man, (B) and I venture that the inscription on the temple at Delphi,* for all its brevity, expresses a precept of greater importance and difficulty than all the thick tomes of moralists. Thus I regard the subject of this discourse as one of the most interesting questions that philosophy can propose and, unfortunately for us, one of the thorniest for philosophers to attempt to resolve. For how can we know the source of inequality among men unless we begin by knowing men themselves? And how will man come to see himself as nature created him, through all the changes that must have been produced in his original constitution in the course of time and events, and how can we separate what he owes to his inborn resources from what circumstances and his advances have added to or changed in his primitive state? Like the statue of Glaucus* so disfigured by time, the sea, and storms as to look less like a god than a wild beast, the human soul modified in society by innumerable constantly recurring causes—the acquisition of a mass of knowledge and a multitude of errors, changes that took place in the constitution of the body, the constant onslaught of the passions—has, as it were, so changed its appearance as to be nearly unrecognizable. And instead of a being that always acts in accordance with certain and invariable principles, instead of that celestial and majestic simplicity the Creator imprinted on it, we find nothing but the deformed contrast between passion mistaken for reason and an understanding in the grip of delirium.

What is crueller yet is that, since all the advances of the human race continually move it ever further from its primitive state, the more new knowledge we accumulate, the more we deprive ourselves of the means for acquiring the most important knowledge of all. Thus, in a sense, it is by studying man that we have made ourselves incapable of knowing him.

It is easy to see that if we are to determine the origin of the differences that now exist among men, we must seek it in these successive changes of the human constitution. Men naturally are, by common consent, as equal among themselves as were the animals of each species before various physical causes introduced into certain species the varieties that we observe. Indeed, it is inconceivable that the first changes, no matter what produced them, should have altered all the individuals of the species all at once and in the same way. But while some men improved or declined, and acquired various good or bad features that were not inherent in their nature, others remained longer in their original state. And such was the earliest source of inequality among men. It is easier to show this in a general way than to determine its exact causes.

Let my readers not then suppose that I am claiming to have seen what seems so difficult to see. I have begun a few lines of reasoning and ventured a few guesses, less in the hope of answering the question than for the purpose of clarifying it and reducing it to its true proportions. Others can easily proceed further along the same path without its being effortless for anyone to reach the end, for it is no small undertaking to separate what is inborn from what is artificial in the present nature of man, to have a proper understanding of a state that no longer exists and perhaps never did and probably never will, but about which we should nevertheless have accurate notions in order to judge our present state properly. Someone who set out to determine the exact precautions to take so as to make valid observations on this subject would need even more philosophy than one might think. And a good solution of the following problem seems to me not unworthy of the Aristotles and Plinys of our own time. 'By what experiments could we gain a knowledge of natural man? And how could these experiments be carried out in society?' Far from attempting to resolve this problem, I believe I have sufficiently reflected on the subject to state in advance that the greatest philosophers would be none too good to direct these experiments, nor the most powerful sovereigns to carry them out, but it is hardly reasonable to expect such a combination, especially in view of the perseverance, or rather the confluence of enlightenment and good will, needed on both sides to achieve success.

Little thought has so far been given to this difficult research, yet it is the only means left to us for clearing up a host of difficulties that conceal the knowledge of the real foundations of human society. It is this ignorance of the nature of man that casts so much uncertainty and obscurity on the true definition of natural right. For the idea of right, says M. Burlamaqui,* and even more that of natural right, are clearly related to the nature of man. Therefore, he continues, the principles of this right must be deduced from that very nature of man, from man's constitution and state.

It is not without a sense of surprise and shock that we observe the lack of agreement prevailing on this important subject among the various authors who have discussed it. Among the most serious writers we find scarcely two who are of the same opinion. Without speaking of the ancient philosophers, who seem to have made it their business to contradict each other on the most fundamental principles, the Roman jurists indiscriminately subjected man and all other animals to the same natural law, because they took this term to mean the law that nature imposes on itself rather than the one that it prescribes, or rather, because of the special sense in which they understood the word 'law', which they seem to have taken only as the expression of the general relations established by nature among all living beings for their common preservation. The moderns mean by the word 'law' only a rule prescribed for a moral being, that is to say, a being that is intelligent, free, and considered in terms of his relation to other beings, and they have consequently limited the application of natural law to the only animal endowed with reason, that is, to man. Since each of them defines natural law in his own way, however, they all establish it on principles so metaphysical that even among us very few people can understand the principles, let alone discover them on their own. All the definitions of these learned men, otherwise in endless contradiction, have one thing in common: that it is impossible to understand the law of nature,* and consequently to obey it, without being a skilled reasoner and a profound metaphysician, which means that for the establishment of society, men must have used the kind of understanding that is developed only with great effort and by a very few people within society itself.

Since we have so little knowledge of nature and since we have so much trouble agreeing on the meaning of the word 'law', it would be extremely hard to agree on a common definition of natural law. Thus all the definitions we find in books, aside from a lack of uniformity, have the added fault of being drawn from several areas of knowledge that men do not naturally possess, and from advantages that they cannot begin to imagine until after they have emerged from the state of nature. Writers begin by searching for the rules on which it would be appropriate for men to agree for the common welfare; and then they give the name 'natural law' to this collection of rules with no other proof than the good that presumably would result from their universal observance. Surely this is a very convenient way of composing definitions and of explaining the nature of things by virtually arbitrary conventions about what is proper.

As long as we have so little understanding of natural man, however, it will be futile for us to try to determine the law he received or the one best suited to his constitution. All that we can clearly see about this law is that for it to be law, not only must the will of the person who is bound by it be capable of submitting to it knowingly, but also, for it to be natural, it must speak directly through the voice of nature.

Leaving aside all the learned books that teach us only to see men as they have made themselves, and reflecting on the first and simplest operations of the human soul, I think I perceive in it two principles that are prior to reason, one of which makes us passionately interested in our well-being and self-preservation, and the other of which inspires in us a natural repugnance for seeing any sentient creature, especially our fellow man, suffer or die. Our minds' ability to co-ordinate and combine these two principles, with no need here to introduce the principle of sociability,* is the source of all the rules of natural right—rules that reason is later forced to re-establish on other foundations when, through its successive developments, it has succeeded in smothering nature.

On this view, one is not obliged to make man a philosopher before making him a man. His duties to others are not uniquely dictated to him by the belated lessons of wisdom; and as long as he does not resist the inner impulse of compassion, he will never do evil to another person or even to any other sentient being except in the legitimate cases where, if his preservation is involved, he is obliged to favour his own. In this way, an end can also be made to the ancient dispute about the participation of animals in natural law, for it is clear that, lacking intelligence and freedom, they cannot recognize this law; since, however, they share to some extent in our nature by virtue of their having sensations, it will be judged that they must also participate in natural right, and that man is subject to some kind of duties toward them. Indeed, it seems that if I am obligated to do no evil to my fellow man, it is less because he is a rational being than because he is a sentient being—a property that, because it is common to both animals and men, should at least give the beast the right not to be needlessly mistreated by man.

This same study of original man, of his true needs and the fundamental principle of his duties, is also the only effective means for doing away with the host of difficulties that present themselves regarding the origin of moral inequality, the true foundations of the body politic, the reciprocal rights of its members, and countless other similar matters whose importance is equalled only by their obscurity.

Human society viewed with a calm and dispassionate gaze seems at first to exhibit only the violence of powerful men and the oppression of the weak. The mind rebels against the harshness of the former; one is inclined to lament the blindness of the latter. And since nothing is less stable among men than those external relationships produced more often by chance than wisdom, and which are called weakness or power, wealth or poverty, human institutions appear at first glance founded on shifting sands. It is only on closer examination, only after clearing away the dust and sand surrounding the edifice, that we perceive the unshakeable base on which it has been built and learn to respect its foundations. Without a serious study of man, his natural faculties, and their successive modifications, we shall never succeed in making these distinctions and in separating, in the present constitution of things, what the divine will has done from what human art has claimed to have done. The political and moral investigations occasioned by the important question I am examining are therefore useful in every way, and the hypothetical history of governments is an instructive lesson for man in every respect. In considering what we would have become if left to ourselves, we must learn to bless him whose beneficent hand, by correcting our institutions and giving them an unshakeable foundation, has prevented the disorders that would otherwise result from them, and has brought forth our happiness from the means that seemed likely to overwhelm us with misery.

Quem te Deus esse
Jussit, et humana qua parte locatus es in re, Disce.*

REMARK ABOUT THE NOTES

To this book I have appended some notes according to my lazy practice of working in fits and starts. These notes sometimes stray far enough from the subject as not to be suitable for reading along with the main text. Hence I have put them at the end of this discourse, in which I have tried my best to follow a straight course. Those with the enterprise to begin again can amuse themselves the second time by beating the bushes and attempt to go through the notes; there will be little ill done if others do not read them at all.

Question
proposed by the Academy of Dijon

What is the origin of inequality among men
and is it warranted by natural law?

DISCOURSE ON THE ORIGIN AND FOUNDATIONS OF INEQUALITY AMONG MEN

I SHALL be speaking of man, and the issue I discuss tells me that I shall be speaking to men, for such questions are not raised by persons who are afraid to acknowledge the truth. Thus, I confidently defend humanity's cause before the men of wisdom who have invited me to do so, and I would not be displeased with myself if I prove worthy of my subject and my critics.

The human species has, I think, two sorts of inequality: the one I call natural or physical because it is established by nature, and consists of differences in age, health, physical strength, and traits of the mind or soul; the other kind we can call moral or political inequality, for it depends on a sort of convention and is established, or at least sanctioned, by the consent of men. This inequality consists of the various privileges that some persons enjoy at the expense of others— such as being wealthier, more honoured, and more powerful than others, and even getting themselves obeyed by others.

One cannot ask what the source of natural inequality is because the answer is expressed by the very definition of the word. Still less can one enquire whether there is not some essential connection between the two kinds of inequality, for that would be to ask, in other words, whether those who command are necessarily worthier than those who obey, and whether bodily or intellectual vigour, wisdom, and virtue are always to be found in individuals in proportion to their power or wealth—possibly a good question to raise among slaves in the hearing of their masters, but one not applicable to free and reasonable men in search of the truth.

So what, precisely, is the subject of this discourse? To pinpoint the moment in the development of events when right replaced violence and nature was subjected to law, and to explain by what sequence of marvellous events the strong could resolve to serve the weak and the people to purchase a semblance of peace at the price of true felicity.

Philosophers examining the foundations of society have all felt the need to go back to the state of nature, but not one of them has managed to reach it. Some have not hesitated to assume that man in that state possessed a notion of the just and the unjust, without bothering to show that he must have had such a concept or that he would even find it useful. Others have spoken of the natural right of each person to keep what belongs to him without saying what they mean by 'belong'. Still others begin by giving the strongest persons authority over the weaker ones, and straightaway introduced government without thinking of the time that had to elapse before the words 'authority' and 'government' could have any meaning among men. All these philosophers, in short, constantly talking of need, greed, oppression, desires, and pride have imported into the state of nature ideas they had taken from society. They talk of savage man and they depict civilized man. Doubts about the quondam existence of a state of nature have never entered most philosophers' heads, yet a reading of the Scriptures plainly reveals that the first man, immediately on receiving the light of reason and the commandments of God, was not himself in this state and that giving the writings of Moses the credence that every Christian philosopher owes them, it must be denied that men were in the pure state of nature even before the Flood, unless through some extraordinary circumstance they reverted to it—a paradox that would be scarcely defensible and quite impossible to prove.

Let us begin by setting aside all the facts,* for they have no bearing on this question. This kind of enquiry is not like the pursuit of historical truth, but depends solely on hypothetical and conditional reasoning, better suited to illuminate the nature of things than to show their actual origin, reasoning similar to that done every day by physicists to explain the formation of the world. Religion commands us to believe that because God took men out of the state of nature†, it was

---

† immediately after Creation   *Added 1782.*

his will that they be unequal, but this does not forbid us to make conjectures based solely on the nature of man and the beings around him, concerning what the human race might have become if it had been left to itself. That, then, is what has been asked of me and what I propose to examine in this discourse. Because my subject concerns man in general, I shall try to use terms intelligible to every nation or rather, forgetting time and place in order to think only of the men I am addressing, I shall imagine myself in the Lyceum of Athens, repeating the lessons of my teachers, with a Plato and Xenocrates as my judges and the human race as my audience.

O Man, listen, whatever be your country and your opinions: here, as I have read it, is your history, not in the books of your fellow men, who lie, but in nature which never lies. Everything issuing from nature is true; nothing in it is false except what I myself have inadvertently put in of my own. The times of which I speak are very remote—how much you have changed from what you once were! I shall, as it were, describe the life of your species, in light of the characteristics you once received which your education and habits could corrupt but not entirely destroy. There is, I think, an age at which the individual would like to go on unchanged; you are going to seek the age at which you would wish your whole species had remained. Dissatisfied with your present condition for reasons that presage even greater unhappiness for your unfortunate posterity, you might wish you could go back in time—and this sentiment must elicit the eulogy of your earliest ancestors, the censure of your contemporaries, and the fright of those who have the misfortune to live after you.

PART I

As important as it is, in making a true judgement of man's natural state, to consider him from his origins and examine him, so to speak, in the embryo of his species, I do not propose to trace his organic system through all its successive developments. I shall not pause to search the animal system for what he might have been at the beginning in order to become what he is at the end. I shall not wonder whether man's elongated nails were, as Aristotle thought, originally hooked claws, whether his body was covered with hair like a bear, or whether walking on all fours (C) with his gaze directed at the earth and his vision confined to several paces did not shape the character and limits of his ideas. On this subject I could form only vague and almost wholly fanciful conjectures; comparative anatomy has as yet made too little progress, and the observations of naturalists are still too uncertain to provide a basis for solid reasoning. Thus, without having recourse to the supernatural knowledge that we have on this subject and without regard to the changes that must have occurred in man's internal and external structure as he put his limbs to new uses and fed himself on new kinds of food, I shall suppose him to have been at all times formed as I see him today, walking on two feet, using his hands in the same way we do, casting his gaze over all nature, and measuring with his eyes the vast expanse of the heavens.

In stripping the creature thus constituted of all the supernatural endowments he may have received and all the artificial faculties that he could have acquired only through a long process, and considering him, in short, as he must have emerged from the hands of nature, I see an animal less strong than some, less agile than others, but on the whole the most advantageously constituted of all. I see him eating his fill under an oak tree, quenching his thirst at the first stream, making his bed at the base of the same tree that supplied his meal, and, behold, his needs are met.

The earth, left to its natural fertility (D) and bespread with immense forests never hewn by an axe, everywhere offers storehouses and shelter for animals of every species. Scattered among the beasts, man observes and imitates their activities and so raises himself to the level of their instincts, with the added advantage that though every other species has only its own instinct, man, who perhaps has none peculiar to himself, arrogates them all and nourishes himself equally well on most of the various foods (E) that the other animals divide among themselves, and he thus finds his sustenance more easily than do any of the rest.

Accustomed from infancy to bad weather and the harshness of the seasons, inured to fatigue, and forced naked and unarmed to defend themselves and their prey from other wild beasts or to escape them by running, men develop a robust and nearly unalterable constitution. Children, coming into the world with the excellent physique of their fathers, and strengthening it by the same exercises that produced it, thus acquire all the vigour of which the human race is capable. Nature treats them precisely the way the law of Sparta treated the children of its citizens: it makes those who are well constituted strong and robust and lets the others perish, differing in this respect from our own societies, in which the state, by making children a burden to their parents, kills them indiscriminately before they are born.

Because a savage's body is the only tool he knows, he puts it to various uses for which our own bodies, for lack of exercise, are unfit; our activities rob us of the strength and agility that necessity obliges him to acquire. If he had had an axe, would his arm have been able to break such solid branches? If he had had a slingshot, would his hand have been able to cast a stone with such speed? If he had had a ladder, would he have been able to climb up a tree so nimbly? If he had had a horse, would he have been able to run so speedily? Give the civilized man the time to assemble all his devices around him, and he will no doubt easily surpass the savage, but if you would like to see an even more unequal match, pit the two naked and unarmed against each other, and you will soon see the advantage of having all one's strength constantly available, of being ever ready for any eventuality, and of always carrying, so to speak, one's whole self with one. (F)

Hobbes claims that man is naturally fearless and seeks only to attack and fight.* On the other hand, an illustrious philosopher* thinks, and Cumberland and Pufendorf agree, that nothing is so timorous as man in the state of nature, ever twitching and ready to flee at the slightest noise he hears or the slightest movement he sees. This may well be true concerning things he does not know, and I have no doubt that he is frightened by every new sight that greets him whenever he cannot discern the physical good or evil he can expect from it, nor compare his strength against the dangers in store—rare circumstances in the state of nature, where all things proceed so uniformly and where the earth's surface is not subject to those abrupt and continual changes caused by the passions and the inconstancy of people living together. The savage, however, living among the animals and soon finding himself in a position to pit himself against them, soon compares himself to them, and noticing that he outstrips them in adroitness more than they do him in strength, learns not to fear them. Set a bear or a wolf against a robust, agile savage—courageous as they all are—armed with stones and a stout stick, and you will see that the danger will be at least reciprocal, and that after several such experiences, wild beasts, which are disinclined to attack their own kind, will also be unwilling to attack man, whom they find just as ferocious as they themselves. With regard to animals with greater strength than he has cunning, man is like other, weaker species that nevertheless subsist, with this advantage, that being no less swift at running than they, and finding almost certain refuge in the trees, he may take on or leave any encounter, and make the choice between flight or combat. Add, too, that it appears that no animal naturally makes war on man except in self-defence or extreme hunger, or exhibits any of those violent antipathies toward man that seem to indicate that one species is destined by nature to be the food of the other.†

† This no doubt explains why Negroes and savages are so unconcerned by the wild animals they encounter in the woods. In this regard, the Caribs of

Man's other and much more fearsome enemies against which he lacks the same means of defending himself are the natural infirmities—infancy, old age, and illnesses of every kind—the doleful evidence of our own frailty, of which the first two are common to all animals, and of which the third belongs principally to man living in society. As for infancy, I notice that the human mother, carrying her child with her everywhere, can nourish it much more easily than do the females of several other species, which are constantly forced to come and go in great fatigue to look for food in one place and to suckle or feed their young in another. It is true if the human mother perishes, her child is in great danger of perishing with her, but this risk is common to a hundred other species whose young are long unable to find their nourishment on their own. And though childhood lasts longer among us, our lives are longer as well, so that on this score things are more or less the same, (G) although there are other principles governing the duration of childhood and the number of young (H) which are not relevant to the present subject. Among old people, who are less active and sweat little, the need for food diminishes along with the ability to procure it—and because the savage's life spares him gout and rheumatism, and because old age is of all ills the one that human assistance can least alleviate, savages expire in the end without anyone noticing that they have ceased to exist and almost without noticing it themselves.

With regard to illnesses, I shall not belabour the false and pointless ranting of most healthy people against medicine, but I ask whether any solid evidence exists for concluding that in the countries where medicine is most rudimentary, the average life of men is shorter than it is in the countries where this art is most carefully practised. And how could this be so if we bring upon ourselves more diseases than medicine can supply remedies? The extreme inequality of the manner of living, the immoderate idleness among some persons and the

Venezuela live among others in the profoundest security and without the least trouble. Though they are all but naked, says François Coréal,* they do not hesitate to show themselves boldly in the woods, armed only with a bow and arrow; but one has never heard of any of them being devoured by beasts. *Added 1782.*

inordinate labour of others, the ease of stimulating and gratifying our appetites and sensual desires, the overrefined food of the rich, which stokes them with constipating sauces and prostrates them with indigestion, the bad food of the poor, which more often than not they lack so greedily gorge it down at every chance; late nights, excesses of every kind, unbridled transports of all the passions, fatigue and exhaustion of the mind, the innumerable sorrows and troubles felt in every class and by which the soul is perpetually tormented: these are the grievous proof that most of our ills are of our own making, nearly all of which we might have avoided by preserving the simple, unchanging, and solitary way of life prescribed for us by nature. If nature has destined us to be healthy, I would almost venture to assert that the state of reflection is contrary to nature and that the man who meditates is a perverse animal. When we think of the good constitution of savages—at least of those we have not devastated with our hard spirits—and realize that they have almost no afflictions except wounds and old age, we are much inclined to believe that the history of human ailments could be written by tracing that of civilized societies. Such was at least the opinion of Plato,* who judged, on the basis of certain remedies used or approved by Podalirius and Machaon during the siege of Troy, that the various illnesses that could be caused by these remedies, were not then known to mankind.† With so few sources of disease, man in the state of nature has little need for remedies and even less for doctors, and in this regard the human race is in no worse condition than any other species and we can easily learn from hunters whether on their expeditions they find many sick animals. Several have been found, many with serious but fully healed wounds, or bones and even limbs broken and fixed by no other surgeon than time and no other regimen than their everyday life, without being any the less perfectly healed for not having been tormented by incisions, poisoned with drugs, or emaciated from fasting. In short, however valuable properly administered medicine may be for us, it is none the less certain that though an ailing savage left on his

† Celsus* reports that dieting, so necessary today, was first invented by Hippocrates. *Added 1782.*

own has nothing to hope for except from nature, conversely he has nothing to fear except his disease, which often makes his situation preferable to ours.

Let us thus guard against confusing savage man with the men we have before our eyes. Nature treats every animal left to its care with a marked partiality that seems to show how jealous it is of this right. The horse, the cat, the bull, and even the donkey are generally larger in size and all have a more robust constitution, more energy, strength, and spiritedness than they do under our roofs. When they are domesticated, they lose half these advantages, and it could be said that all our efforts to treat and feed these animals have only succeeded in making them degenerate. The same is true even of man himself; in becoming sociable and a slave, he becomes weak, fearful, and obsequious; his soft, effeminate way of life ends up draining him of both strength and courage. Furthermore, the difference between the savage and the domesticated man must be greater than the difference between wild animals and tame animals, for since nature has treated men and beasts alike, the conveniences man creates for himself beyond those he gives to the animals he tames must cause him to degenerate more appreciably.

For these first men, being naked, unhoused, and bereft of all those useless things we believe so necessary is no great misfortune and especially no great obstacle to their survival. If their skins are devoid of hair, they have no need of it in warm regions and in chilly climes they soon learn to wear the skins of the animals they have overpowered. If they have but two legs for running, they have two arms for self-defence and the provision of their needs; their children may perhaps learn to walk, belatedly and stumblingly, but their mothers can easily carry them, an advantage lacking in other species, where the mother, when pursued, is forced to abandon her young or to adjust her pace to theirs.[†] Finally, unless we

---

[†] There may be some exceptions to this: for example, the animal in the province of Nicaragua that resembles a fox, with feet like a man's hands and, according to Coréal, a pouch under its belly where the mother puts her young whenever she is obliged to flee. This is doubtless the same animal that in Mexico is called the 'tlaquatzin', the female of which is said by Laët[*] to have a similar pouch for the same purpose. *Added 1782.*

assume these singular and fortuitous confluences of circumstances (of which I shall speak further on), ones that could well never happen, it is clear in any case that the first man who made himself clothes and a lodging was supplying himself with things that were hardly necessary, for he had hitherto done without them and it is hard to see why as a grown man he could not tolerate the kind of life he had tolerated since his infancy.

Solitary, idle, and never far from danger, the savage must love to sleep, but he must sleep lightly, like animals, which think little and may be said to sleep whenever they are not thinking. Because the savage's self-preservation is almost his sole concern, his best-developed faculties must be those devoted mainly to attack or defence: to overpower a prey or to avoid becoming the prey of another animal. On the other hand, the organs that develop only through softness and sensuality must remain rudimentary, precluding any kind of delicacy; and because his senses are divided in this way, his sense of touch and taste are extremely crude, but his sight, hearing, and smell are very acute. What is true of animals in general is, according to the reports of explorers, true of most savage peoples as well. Thus we should not be surprised that the Hottentots of the Cape of Good Hope sight with the naked eye ships on the high seas at as great a distance as the Dutch see with their telescopes, or that the savages of America scent Spaniards on the trail as well as do the best dogs; or that all these barbarous nations comfortably accept their nakedness or that they sharpen their taste with peppers and drink strong European spirits like water.

Up to this point, I have considered only the physical man; let us look at his metaphysical and moral sides.

I see in every animal merely an ingenious machine to which nature has given senses to keep it going by itself and to protect itself, up to a certain point, from everything likely to distress or annihilate it. I see precisely the same things in the human machine, with the difference that nature alone does everything in the activities of a beast while man contributes to his own, in his capacity as a free agent. The beast chooses or rejects by instinct, man by free action, meaning that the beast cannot deviate from the rule prescribed for it, even when it might benefit from doing so, whereas man often deviates from such laws to his own detriment. That is why a pigeon would die of hunger next to a dish filled with choice meats and a cat next to a heap of fruit or grain, even though either of them could get nourishment from the foods it disdains if it only had thought of trying them. Thus, dissolute men give themselves over to excesses that bring on fevers and death, because the mind perverts the senses and the will continues to speak when nature is silent.

Every animal has ideas because it has senses, and even combines these ideas up to a certain point; in this respect man differs from the beast only in degree. Some philosophers have suggested that there is a greater difference between one man and another than between a given man and a given beast. Thus it is not his understanding that constitutes the distinctive characteristic of man among all other animals, but his capacity as a free agent. Nature commands every animal, and the beast obeys. Man experiences the same impulsion, but he recognizes that he is free to comply or resist; and it is above all the awareness of this freedom that reveals the spirituality of his soul, for physics in some way explains the mechanism of the senses and the formation of ideas, but in the power of willing, or rather choosing, and in our sense of this power, we find purely mental acts wholly inexplicable by the laws of mechanics.

Although the difficulties surrounding all these questions leave some room for disagreement about this difference between man and beast, there is one further highly specific, distinctive, and indisputable feature of man, and that is his faculty of self-improvement—a faculty that, with the help of circumstances, successively develops all the others and that in man inheres as much in the species as in the individual, whereas an animal at the end of a few months already is what it will remain all its life, and its species will be at the end of a thousand years what it was in the first of those thousand years. Why is only man prone to turn senile? Is it not the case that he thus returns to his primitive state and that, while the beast that has acquired nothing and hence has nothing to lose is always left with its instincts, man, losing through old age or some accident all that his *perfectibility**has enabled him to acquire, thus sinks lower than the beast? It would be sad for us to be forced to admit that this distinctive and nearly unlimited faculty was the source of all man's unhappiness and, in time, draws him out of that primordial condition in which he would savour peaceful and innocent days; and that it was this faculty, causing over the centuries his acumen and his errors, his vices and virtues to flourish, which eventually makes man a tyrant over himself and nature. (I) It would be appalling to be obliged to praise as a beneficent creature the man who first suggested to the inhabitants of the banks of the Orinoco the practice of flattening their infants'. temples with boards and so ensuring them of at least a part both of their imbecility and original happiness.

The savage man, consigned by nature to instinct alone—or rather compensated for the instinct he may lack by faculties that can replace it at first and later raise him far above nature—begins with purely animal functions; (J) his earliest state will be perception and feeling, experiences shared by every other animal. Willing and unwilling, desiring and fearing, will be his soul's first and just about only operations until new circumstances cause it to undergo new developments.

Whatever moralists say about it, the human understanding owes a great deal to the passions, which, by common consent, also owe a great deal to the understanding. Reason develops through the activity of the passions; we seek to know only because we wish to enjoy, and it is inconceivable that a man who had neither fears nor desires would bother to reason. The passions, in turn, originate in our needs and owe their progress to our knowledge, for we can desire or fear things only if we can form some ideas of them in our mind or through a simple impulse of nature. The savage, lacking any sort of enlightenment, experiences passions only of the latter kind; his desires do not go beyond his physical needs; (K) the only goods in the world he knows are food, a female, and repose, and the only evils he fears are pain and hunger. I say pain and not death, for an animal will never know what it is to die, and a knowledge of death and its terrors is one of man's first acquisitions upon leaving the animal condition.

It would be easy for me, if necessary, to support this belief by facts, and to show how among all the nations of the world, the mind's progress is exactly proportionate to the needs that their peoples received from nature or those imposed on them by circumstances, and consequently to the passions that led them to provide for their needs. I would show how the arts sprang up in Egypt, and spread with the overflowing waters of the Nile; I would follow their progress in ancient Greece, where they took on new life, grew, and rose to the heavens among the sand and rocks of Attica without being able to take root on the banks of the Eurotas. I would observe that the peoples of the North show generally more industriousness than those of the South because they are less able to forego this attribute, as though nature had chosen to equal things out by giving men's minds the fertility it denied the soil.

Without recourse to the uncertain evidence of history, however, who does not see that everything seems to remove the savage man from the temptation and the means to leave the savage condition? His imagination portrays nothing; his heart yearns for nothing; his modest needs are easily within reach; and he is so far from having sufficient knowledge to wish to acquire even more that he can have neither foresight nor curiosity. Nature's spectacle becomes so familiar that it leaves him indifferent. There is always the same pattern, there are always the same revolutions. He lacks the intellect to wonder at the greatest marvels and it is not to him that we should look for the philosophy man needs if he is to know how to observe at some point what he has seen every day. His soul, perturbed by nothing, is concerned only with the sense of his current existence, with no idea of the future, however near, and his plans, as limited as his horizon, barely extend to the end of the day. Even today, such is the foresight of a Caribbean Indian:* in the morning he sells his cotton bed and returns weeping to buy it back in the evening, having failed to foresee he would need it for the coming night.

The more we reflect on this subject, the greater the distance seems between pure sensations and the simplest knowledge, and it is inconceivable how a man on his strength alone, without the help of communication or the spur of necessity, could bridge so great a gap. How many centuries must have elapsed before men were in a position to see any other fire than that in the sky overhead? How many chance occurrences were needed to teach them the commonest uses of this element? How many times did they let their fires go out before people learned how to rekindle them? And how many times did the knowledge of these secrets die with the one who had discovered it? What are we to say of agriculture, an art that demands much industry and foresight, which depends on other arts, and is obviously practicable only where society has at least begun and an art that we use not so much to procure foods from the earth, which could provide them plentifully without our help, but rather to force it to produce those more to our taste. Let us suppose, however, that men became so numerous that the natural produce no longer sufficed to feed them—a supposition that, we may remark in passing, would show this way of life to be highly beneficial for the human species. Suppose that, without forges or workshops, farming tools had fallen from the heavens into the hands of savages, and that they had overcome the mortal dread that all men feel toward constant labour; suppose they learned to anticipate their needs so far in advance that they had guessed how to cultivate the soil, sow seeds, and plant trees; that they had discovered the art of milling grain and fermenting grapes—all things that the gods would have had to teach them, for it is inconceivable that they could have learned them on their own. After all this, what man would be so demented as to break his back cultivating a field only to have it stripped bare by the first comer—man or beast—enticed by the crop! And can any man resolve to spend his life in irksome toil when the greater his need of the rewards of this, the surer he is of losing them? In short, how can this situation drive men to cultivate the land unless it was parcelled out among them, that is, unless the state of nature has been eradicated?

Even if we wish to assume that savage man was as proficient in the art of thinking as our philosophers portray him; even if, following their example, we made him a philosopher as well, discovering on his own the most sublime truths and, by a process of highly abstract reasoning, formulating for himself maxims of justice and reason derived from the love of order in general or the known will of his Creator; in short, even if we assumed his mind to be as intelligent and enlightened as it is actually dull and stupid, what value would a species find in this metaphysics that was incommunicable and would perish along with the man who invented it? What progress would the human race make scattered among the animals in the woods? And how much could men better themselves and find mutual enlightenment when, without fixed dwellings or any need for each other, they might meet up scarcely twice in their lives, without recognizing or speaking to each other?

Let us bear in mind how many ideas we owe to the use of speech, how much grammar facilitates and trains the operations of the mind. Let us think of the incredible exertion and infinite time that the original invention of language must have cost. Put these thoughts together, and you may imagine how many thousands of centuries were required for the successive development of all the operations of which the mind is capable.

Allow me a brief consideration of the obstacles to the origin of languages. I could be content to cite or repeat the research the abbé de Condillac* has done on this subject, all of which fully confirms my thoughts and indeed may have given me my first ideas about this. Since, however, the way this philosopher resolves the difficulties he creates for himself on the origin of words shows that he assumes what I call into question, namely some sort of already established society among the inventors of language, I think that I should put my own thoughts together with his to explain these difficulties in terms best suited to my own subject. The first problem is that of imagining how language could have become necessary, for because men had no dealings with each other or indeed no need for any, the necessity or indeed the possibility of language is inconceivable, if it could be done without. Like many others, I could say languages were born of the domestic interchanges of fathers, mothers, and children, but that would not only fail to meet the difficulties, but also repeat the mistake of those who explain the state of nature with ideas imported from civil society; they always see the family gathered under the same roof, its members preserving among themselves a cohesion as intimate and permanent as those we do ourselves, in which many common interests unite them, whereas among peoples in this primitive condition, without houses or huts or property of any kind, each person took shelter where he happened to find himself, often for one night only; males and females united seren-dipitously, according to chance encounters, opportunity, and desire, without any great need for speech to express the things they had to say to each other, and they went their separate ways with the same readiness. (L) Initially, the mother nursed her children to satisfy her own needs, but then habit endeared them to her and she fed to satisfy theirs; when they were strong enough to find their own food, they soon left their mother, and because nearly the only way to meet up again was to keep each other in sight, they soon reached the point of not even recognizing one another. Observe that because the child has all his needs to express and hence more things to say to his mother than she has to say to him, the child must bear the brunt of inventing language, and the language he uses must be largely of his own making—all of which would bring into being as many languages as there are individuals speaking them. This is further compounded by a roving, vagabond life that would leave no time for any language to stabilize: for to say that the mother articulates for the child the words he is to use to ask her for this or that object shows well enough how already existing languages are taught, but does not show how languages are formed in the first place.

Suppose that this first difficulty has been overcome, and we can vault for a moment over the broad gap between the pure state of nature and the need for language, and let us enquire—assuming them necessary (M)—how languages could initially be constructed. Here, we come across a fresh difficulty, worse still than the previous one, for if men needed speech to learn to think, they needed still more to know how to think in order to discover the art of speaking; and when we understood how vocal sounds came to be taken as the conventional expressions of our ideas, the problem would still remain of explaining what the conventional expressions may have been for ideas that have no tangible objects and hence could not be indicated by gesture or voice, so that we are hard put to formulate tenable conjectures about the birth of this art of communicating our thoughts and establishing an interchange between minds—this sublime art that is now so remote from its origins, but that the philosopher still sees at such a prodigious distance from its perfection that no man would be audacious enough to claim that it would ever get there, even if the revolutions time necessarily brings were suspended in its favour, and prejudices deserted the academies or fell silent before them, and even if those academies could study this thorny topic for centuries without stopping.

Man's first language, the most universal and forceful language, and the only one he needed before he had to persuade gatherings of other men, was the cry of nature. Because this cry was wrenched from him only by a kind of instinct at times of acute urgency, to plead for help in great perils or for relief from terrible afflictions, it was not widely used in ordinary life, where more moderate feelings prevail. When men's thoughts spread and multiplied, and closer personal relations were established among them, they sought a greater number of signs and a more comprehensive language. They augmented their vocal inflections and combined them with gestures, which are naturally more expressive and whose meaning is less dependent on some prior agreement. Thus, gestures were made to express moving and visible things, and imitative sounds made for audible things. Because, however, gestures can only indicate objects that are actually present or easily described and actions that are visible; and because gestures are not universally effective, however, being rendered useless by darkness or the inter-position of a screening object, and requiring rather than arousing the attention of others, men eventually thought of substituting vocal articulations, which, without having the same relation to certain ideas, are better for representing them all as words or conventional signs. This substitution could only have been made by common consent and in a way rather difficult to put into practice by men whose crude organs had not yet been trained, and even more difficult to conceive of in itself, for such unanimous agreement would need to be justified and the power of speech seems to have been absolutely necessary in order to establish the use of speech.

We must assume that the first words men used had a much broader meaning in their minds than do words employed in languages already formed; and that because men were ignorant of the division of discourse into its constituent parts, they first gave each word the meaning of a whole sentence. When they began distinguishing subject from predi-cate, and verbs from nouns, which itself was no mean achievement, substantives were at first just so many proper names, the tense of all verbs was the infinitive,[†] and the notion of adjectives must have developed with considerable difficulty, for every adjective is an abstract word, and abstracting is an irksome and rather unnatural operation.

At first, each object was given a particular name, without regard to genera and species, which these first founders of language were unable to tell apart; and all particular things appeared isolated in men's minds as they are in the spectacle of nature. If one oak was called A, another oak was called B,[‡] so that the more limited their knowledge, the thicker their dictionary. The burden in all this nomenclature could not easily be eliminated, for to put things under common and generic denominations, one had to be acquainted with their properties and differences; observations and definitions were

---

[†] the present infinitive   *1782.*

[‡] for the first idea inferred in observing two things is that they are not the same, and it often takes a good deal of time to observe what they have in common   *Added 1782.*

needed, that is, more natural history and metaphysics than men at that time could possibly have known.

Furthermore, general ideas can be introduced into the mind only with the help of words, and the understanding grasps them only through sentences. This is one of the reasons why animals cannot formulate such ideas or acquire the perfectibility that depends on them. When a monkey goes without pause from one nut to another, does anyone think it has a general idea of this sort of fruit and compares the two nuts with an archetype? Certainly not; the sight of one of these nuts calls to its memory the sensation it received from the other, and its eyes, modified in a certain way, signal to its sense of taste the change about to be experienced. Every general idea is purely intellectual; if the imagination is the least involved in it, the idea forthwith becomes particular. Try to draw for yourself the image of a tree in general and you will never succeed; despite yourself, you must see a tree as large or small, bare or leafy, light or dark, and if you could see in it only what is found in every tree, that image would no longer resemble a tree. Purely abstract entities are seen in the same way or are conceivable only by means of language. Only the definition of a triangle gives you a true idea of it; when you picture one in your mind, it is one particular triangle and not another, and you cannot avoid making the lines of it perceptible or its plane coloured. Hence, it is necessary to utter sentences and to speak in order to have general ideas; for when the imagination ceases working, the mind proceeds no further without the support of discourse. Hence, if the first inventors of speech were able to give names to the ideas they already had, it follows that the first nouns must have been proper names.

When, however, our new grammarians began—by what means I cannot conceive—to extend their ideas and generalize their words, the ignorance of these inventors must have put stringent limitations on their method; and because they must have initially produced too many names for particulars out of a lack of knowledge of genera and species, they must later have produced too few of them out of a lack of discrimination between the differences between things.

Extending the division far enough would have required more experience and knowledge than they could have had as well as more study and labour than they would have wished to expend on it. Even now, as we discover each day new species that had hitherto escaped all our observations, imagine how many must have been hidden from men who judged things only by first appearance! As for primary classes and the most general notions, it is superfluous to add that these too must have escaped them. How, for example, would these men have imagined or understood the words 'matter', 'mind', 'substance', 'mode', 'figure', or 'movement', when our philosophers who have long been using them have themselves great difficulty understanding them, and when the ideas connected with these words being purely metaphysical, the words have no models in nature?

I must stop with these first steps, and ask my critics to pause in their reading here to consider, concerning the invention of physical substantives alone, the easiest part of speech to invent, the distance language still has to go before it can express all human thoughts, assume a constant form, be spoken in public,* and have an influence on society. I beg them to reflect on how much time and knowledge were needed to discover numbers, (N) abstract words, aorists and all the verb tenses, particles, syntax, the linking of sentences, the forms of reasoning, and to create all the logic of discourse. For myself, daunted by the myriad difficulties and convinced of the nearly certain impossibility that languages could have been created and established by purely human means, I leave to anyone who will undertake it the discussion of the following difficult problem: Which was more necessary, a previously established society for the invention of language, or a previously invented language for the establishment of society?

Whatever the origins of language may be, it is easy to see at least from the lack of care taken by nature to bring men together through mutual needs, or to make the use of speech easier, how little it prepared them to be sociable or contributed to all they have done to establish their social bonds. Indeed, it is unimaginable why in that primitive state one man would need a fellow man any more than a monkey or a wolf needs its fellow creature, or, assuming he did, what reason could induce the other man to minister to it, or in the latter case, how the two could agree among themselves on the conditions. I know we are repeatedly told* that nothing was so miserable as man in the state of nature; and if it is true, as I believe I have proved, that man could have either the desire or the chance to leave that state only after many centuries, this is an accusation to lodge against nature and not against him whom nature so fashioned. If, however, I understand the term 'miserable' correctly, it is a word that means nothing or merely a painful deprivation and suffering in body or soul. Now I would like to have it explained to me what kind of misery could exist in a free being whose heart is at peace and whose body is healthy: I ask which kind of life—civilized or natural—is more apt to become unbearable to those who experience it? Around us we see people almost all of whom complain of their existence and even several of whom renounce it as much as possible; and divine and human law together do little to arrest this disorder. I wonder whether anyone has ever heard of a free savage who ever dreamt of complaining about his life or killing himself? Let it be judged with less vanity on which side true misery lies. On the contrary, nothing would be as miserable as a savage man dumbfounded by knowledge, tormented by passions, and reasoning about a state different from his own. Thanks to a very wise providence, his potential faculties developed only with the opportunities to use them, so that they were neither superfluous nor prematurely onerous, nor belated and un-availing when they were needed. In instinct alone man had everything he needed to live in the state of nature, and in cultivated reason, he has everything he needs to live in society.

At first glance, it would seem that because in the state of nature men have no kind of moral relationships to each other, nor any recognized duties, they would be neither good nor evil, and could have neither vices nor virtues; unless we took those words in a physical sense and could call an individual's 'vices' those attributes that might be deleterious to his own survival and 'virtues' those that might be propitious for it, in which case we should have to call most virtuous the person who least resisted the simple impulses of nature. But without diverging from ordinary usage, we would do well to suspend judgement on this situation and guard against our own biases until we have observed, with the scales of impartiality in our hands, more virtues than vices among civilized men, whether those men's virtues are more beneficial than their vices are pernicious; or whether the advancement of their knowledge adequately compensates for the harm they do each other, as they learn of the good they should do each other; or whether, all things considered, they would not be in a happier situation, having neither harm to fear from anyone nor good to hope from anyone, rather than subjecting themselves to a universal dependence and obligating themselves to accept everything from those who do not obligate themselves to give them anything.

Above all, let us not conclude with Hobbes that man is naturally wicked because he has no idea of goodness or vice-ridden because he has no knowledge of virtue, that he always withholds from his fellow men services that he does not believe he owes them, or on the strength of his properly claimed right to the things he needs, he madly imagines himself to be the sole owner of the universe. Hobbes clearly saw the flaw in all modern definitions of natural right, but the conclusions he drew from his own definition show that his own concept of natural right is no less false. Reasoning according to his own principles, that writer should have said instead that because the state of nature is the one in which man's concern for his survival least encroaches on that of others, it is the one most conducive to peace and befitting of mankind. He said precisely the opposite as a result of improperly introducing into savage man's concern for his own survival the need to satisfy a host of passions that are the handiwork of society and that have made laws necessary. The wicked man, he said, is a robust child;* it remains to be seen whether savage man is this robust child. Even if we conceded this point to Hobbes, what would he conclude from it? That if this man were as dependent on others when he is robust as when he is weak, there is no kind of excess he would not commit: that he would assault his mother when she delayed nursing him at her breast, that he would strangle one younger brother who annoyed him, or bite the leg of another when struck or otherwise bothered by him. But Hobbes is here making two conflicting suppositions about man in the state of nature: that he is robust and that he is dependent. Man is weak when he is dependent, and becomes emancipated before he is robust. Hobbes did not see that the same cause preventing savages from using their reason (as our jurists claim) also prevents them from abusing their faculties (as Hobbes himself claims), so that it could be said that savages are not wicked precisely because they do not know what it is to be good, for it is neither the development of knowledge nor the restraint of law, but the calm of the passions, and ignorance of vice that keeps them from doing wrong. 'Tanto plus in illis proficit vitiorum ignoratio, quam in his cognitio virtutis.'* There is, moreover, another principle that Hobbes failed to see and that—having been given to man to temper the fierceness of his vanity or his desire for self-preservation before the birth of this vanity (O)—moderates his zeal for his own well-being by an innate aversion to the sight of a fellow creature's suffering. I believe I need have no fear of contradiction when I credit man with the one natural virtue that the most intemperate detractor of human virtues has been forced to recognize.* I speak of pity, a fitting predisposition for creatures as weak and subject to as many ills as we, a virtue all the more universal and useful to man because it precedes any kind of reflection in him, and so natural that even the beasts themselves sometimes show discernible signs of it. Without speaking of the tenderness of mothers for their young and the dangers they brave in order to protect them, we observe every day the aversion of horses to trampling any living body underfoot; an animal never passes a dead creature from its own species without uneasiness; there are even some that give their dead a sort of burial; and the sorrowful lowing of cattle entering a slaughterhouse bespeaks their feelings about the horrible spectacle facing them. One sees with pleasure how the author of *The Fable of the Bees*, forced to recognize man as a sensitive and

compassionate creature, departs from his cold and brittle
style in the example he gives of this, presenting us with the
heart-rending image of a man compelled to behold, from a
place of confinement, a wild beast tear a child from his
mother's breast, crushing the child's fragile limbs with its
murderous fangs and ripping out the quivering entrails with
its claws. What terrible agitation must be felt by this witness
of an event in which he has no personal stake! What agony
he must suffer at seeing this sight, and being unable to do
anything to help the fainting mother or the dying child!

Such is the pure movement of nature, prior to all reflection;
such is the force of natural pity, which the most vicious
immorality still finds hard to overcome—for every day we
see in our theatres persons moved, and even weeping, at the
sufferings of a poor wretch who, were he in the tyrant's
place, would only increase the torments of his enemy.†
Mandeville realized that men, despite all their ethics, would
never be anything more than monsters if nature had not
given them pity to bolster their reason, but he failed to see
that this trait alone is the source of all the social virtues that
he wishes to dispute in man. Indeed, what are generosity,
mercy, and humaneness if not pity accorded to the weak, the
guilty, and the human race in general? Kindliness, and even
friendship, correctly understood, is only the outcome of an
enduring pity for a particular object, for, is wishing a person
not to suffer anything other than wishing him to be happy?
Even if it were true that commiseration is just a feeling
that makes us empathize with the victim, a feeling that is
unnamed but keen in savage man, and well developed but
slight in civilized man, what difference would this make to
the truth of what I am saying, except to make it more

---

† They are like the bloodthirsty Sulla, who was so sensitive to suffering he
was not responsible for, or like Alexander of Pherae, who dared not attend
the performance of any tragedy, lest he be seen sobbing with Andromache
and Priam, although he could listen impassively to the screams of all the
citizens whose throats were cut daily on his orders.

> Mollissima corda
> Humano generi dare se Natura fatetur
> Quae lacrimas dedit* *Added 1782.*

forceful? Indeed, pity becomes stronger as the animal looking on more closely identifies itself with the animal suffering. Clearly, this identification must have been immeasurably more powerful in the state of nature than in the state of reasoning. It is reason that breeds vanity and reflection that strengthens it; reason that turns man inward; reason that separates man from everything that troubles or afflicts him. It is philosophy that isolates him and prompts him secretly to say at the sight of a person suffering: 'Perish if you will, but I am safe.' Now only dangers to the society as a whole will disturb the tranquil sleep of the philosopher and yank him from his bed. Someone may with impunity slit the throat of a fellow man under the philosopher's window, and the philosopher need only put his hands over his ears and argue a bit with himself to prevent nature, which is rebelling inside him, from making him identify himself with the man being murdered. The savage man does not have this commendable talent, and for lack of wisdom and reason he always yields impetuously to the first impulses of human feeling. In riots or street brawls, the crowd always gathers round and the cautious man departs; it is the ill-bred rabble, the market-women, who separate the scufflers and prevent decent people from tearing each other to pieces.

Hence, it is certain that pity is a natural sentiment moderating the action of self-love* in each individual and so contributing to the mutual preservation of the whole species. It is pity that sends us unreflecting to the aid of those we see suffering; it is pity that in the state of nature takes the place of laws, moral habits, and virtues, with the added benefit that there no one is tempted to disobey its gentle voice; it will deter a robust savage from robbing a weak child or infirm old person of his hard-won sustenance if the savage himself can hope to find his own elsewhere; it is pity that, in place of that sublime maxim of rational justice, 'Do unto others as you would have them do unto you,' inspires in all men that other maxim of natural goodness, much less perfect but perhaps more useful: 'Do what is good to yourself with as little possible harm to others.' In short, it is to this natural feeling, rather than to any subtle arguments, that we must look for the cause of the aversion that every man feels to doing evil, quite independently of the maxims of education. Although it may be the business of Socrates and others of that stamp to acquire virtue through reason, the human race would long ago have ceased to exist if its preservation had depended strictly on the reasoning power of the individuals who make it up.

With such dormant passions and such a beneficent check, men who were more wild than evil, and more intent on warding off possible harm to themselves than tempted to do harm to others, were not prone to highly dangerous quarrels. Because they had no kind of dealings with each other, they were consequently unacquainted with vanity, credit, esteem, or contempt; because they had no idea of 'mine' and 'yours', and no real idea of justice; and because they regarded any violence they might suffer as a harm easily redressed rather than an insult to be punished; and because they did not even dream of vengeance, except perhaps mechanically and on the spot, like a dog biting a stone thrown at it, these men's disputes seldom had bloody consequences, provided the issue was no more touchy than food; yet I see a more dangerous issue remains for me to discuss.

Among the passions stirring the human heart, there is one that is burning and impetuous, and makes one sex necessary for the other, a terrible passion that braves every danger, defies every obstacle, and in its fury seems destined to destroy the very human race it is designed to preserve. What will become of men, who are prey to unbridled and brutal rage, without shame, without modesty, without restraint, fighting every day over their loves at the cost of their lives?

First, it must be agreed that the more violent the passions, the more necessary are laws to contain them; but apart from the fact that the disorders and crimes that these passions cause every day among us clearly enough reveal the inadequacy of laws in this regard, it would be good to examine whether these disorders did not arise with the laws themselves; for then, if the laws were capable of suppressing such disorders, the very least that one would demand of them is that they should put a stop to an evil that would not exist without them.

Let us begin by distinguishing the moral from the physical in the sentiment of love. The physical is the universal desire that leads one sex to unite with the other; the moral is what shapes desire and focuses it on a single object, or at least makes the desire for the chosen object more forceful. It is easily seen that the moral side of love is an unnatural sentiment, born of social custom and honoured by women with much care and skill in order to establish their power over men and so make dominant the sex that ought to obey. Because this sentiment is grounded on certain notions of merit and beauty that a savage is not equipped to feel and on comparisons he is not equipped to make, it must be almost non-existent for him. For since his mind cannot form abstract ideas of regularity and proportion, his heart is incapable of feeling those sentiments of love and admiration that—even without its being noticed—issue from the application of these ideas: he heeds only the sexual constitution instilled in him by nature, and not the taste[†] that he is unable to acquire: for him, any woman is good.

Confined solely to the physical side of love and fortunate enough to be unacquainted with those preferences that inflame the urge for it and increase the difficulties of satisfying it, men must experience the ardours of their sexual nature less often and less keenly, and consequently must have fewer and less violent disputes among themselves. Imagination, which wreaks much havoc among us, never speaks to the savage's heart; each one calmly awaits the urge of nature, responds to it automatically, with more pleasure than frenzy, and once the need is satisfied, all desire is extinguished.

It is thus incontestable that only in society has love itself, like all the other passions, acquired that driving intensity that so often makes it fatal to men; and it is all the more ridiculous to portray savages constantly killing each other to satisfy their brutishness, for this idea is directly contrary to

[†] distaste 1782.

experience: the Caribs,* who of all existing peoples have up
to now least strayed from the state of nature, are the most
gentle in their loves, and the least prone to jealousy, despite
their living in the kind of torrid climate that always seems to
spark those passions.

As for the inferences to be drawn from several species
of animals, from the combats between males, which at all
times bloody our farmyards or make our springtime forests
resound with their roars as they fight over females, we must
begin by excluding all species where nature has clearly
established in the comparative strength of the sexes, relations
different from those that exist among us. Thus, cockfights
have no implications for the human species. In species where
the proportions are more balanced, such conflicts can only be
caused by a scarcity of females relative to the number
of males, or to the season of exclusion when the female
continuously spurns the male's advances, which amounts to
the same thing, for when each female tolerates the male only
two months throughout the year, it is as if the population of
females had been reduced by five-sixths. Neither of these two
cases is applicable to the human species, where the number
of females generally exceeds that of males and where no
one has ever observed, even among savages, females having
periods of heat and exclusion like other species. Moreover,
among several of such animals the whole species goes into
heat at the same time, so that there comes a terrible moment
of universal lustfulness, uproar, disorder, and fighting—a
moment that does not occur in the human species, where
love is never cyclical. Therefore the struggles that occur
among certain animals for the possession of the females
provide no grounds for any conclusion about the behaviour
of men in the state of nature; and even if we could draw such
a conclusion, the fact that these conflicts do not destroy the
other species obliges us at least to believe that they would
not be more deadly than ours; and it is very clear that they
would still cause less havoc in the state of nature than they
do in society, particularly in those countries where, since
morals still count for something, the jealousy of lovers and
the vengeance of husbands are the daily cause of duels,

murders, and even worse deeds, and where the duty of eternal fidelity serves only to bring about adultery, and where the laws of chastity and honour necessarily spread debauchery and multiply abortions.

Let us conclude, then, that savage man wandering in the forests, without work, without speech, without a dwelling, without war, and without ties, with no need of his fellow men and no desire to harm them, perhaps not even recognizing any one of them individually, subject to few passions and sufficient unto himself, had only such sentiments and knowledge as were suited to his condition; he felt only his true needs, saw only what he thought it was in his interest to see, and his understanding made no more progress than his vanity. If he happened to make some discovery, he was unable to communicate it to others, for he did not even recognize his own children. Every art perished with its inventor. There was no education or progress; the generations multiplied unproductively, and because each began anew from the same point, centuries passed by in all the crudeness of the earliest ages; the species was already old, and man remained ever a child.

I have dwelt so long on the hypothesis of this primitive condition because, having to overcome age-old errors and entrenched beliefs, I thought it necessary to dig down to the roots, and portray the true state of nature in order to show how inequality, even in its natural form, is far less real and influential there than our writers claim.

In fact, it is easy to see that among the distinctive differences between men there are several that pass for natural but are solely the work of habit and the various ways of life that men adopt in society. Thus, a sturdy or fragile temperament, together with its resultant strength or weakness, is often due more to a strict or effeminate upbringing than to the body's original constitution. The same is true of the strength of the mind, for not only does education determine a difference between minds that are cultivated and those that are not, but it increases the difference between cultivated minds in proportion to their culture; for when a giant and a dwarf walk along the same road, every stride gives a new advantage to the giant. When we compare the great diversity in up-bringing and ways of life that prevail among the various classes in the civil state with the simplicity and uniformity in animal and savage life, where every creature eats of the same foods, lives in the same manner, and does exactly the same things, we understand how much less the difference between man and man must be in the state of nature than in society, and how much natural inequality must have increased in the human species through the effects of institutionalized inequality.

Even if, however, nature did exhibit as much favouritism in dispensing its gifts as is claimed, what advantage would the most highly favoured gain from this at the expense of the others, in a state of affairs that allowed for almost no kind of relationship between them? Where there is no love, of what use would beauty be? Of what use would the intellect be to people who do not speak, or guile to those who have no dealings with others? I hear it constantly repeated that the stronger will oppress the weak, but I would like an explanation of what is meant by 'oppression'. Some men are violently domineering and others groan in abject sub-servience to their whims: that is precisely what I observe among us, but I do not see how that could be said of savage men, who could hardly be brought even to understand what servitude and domination are. A man might well take the fruits that another has plucked, the game he has killed, or the cave he uses as shelter, but how will he ever manage to exact obedience, and what sort of chains of dependence will there be among men who own nothing? If someone chases me away from one tree, I am at liberty to go to another one; if someone harasses me in one place, who will stop me from going elsewhere? Is there a man so much stronger than I and, moreover, perverse, lazy, and brutish enough to force me to provide for his sustenance while he remains idle? He would have to resolve not to let me out of his sight for an instant, and make a point of keeping me tied up while he sleeps, for fear that I might escape or kill him: that is to say, he would be obliged to expose himself voluntarily to much more trouble than the trouble he would wish to avoid, and the trouble he would make for me. After all this, suppose his vigilance momentarily slackens? Suppose an unexpected noise makes him turn his head? I slip twenty paces into the forest, my chains are broken, and he never sees me again in his life.

Without going into these needless details, anyone can see that because the bonds of servitude are formed only through the mutual dependence of men and the reciprocal needs that unite them, it is impossible to enslave a man without first putting him in a state where he cannot do without another man, and since such a situation does not exist in the state of nature, each man there is free of the yoke, and the law of the strongest is nullified.

After proving that inequality is scarcely noticeable in the state of nature, and that its influence there is almost negligible, it remains for me to explain its origin and progress in the successive developments of the human mind. After showing that perfectibility, the social virtues, and other faculties that natural man received as potentialities could never have developed on their own, that to do so they needed the fortuitous convergence of several external causes that might never have arisen and without which man would have forever remained in his primitive condition,[†] it remains for me to bring together and consider the various chance events that might have succeeded in improving human reason while worsening the human species, made man wicked while making him sociable, and led man and the world from their remote beginnings to the point at which we now observe them.

Because the events I am about to describe might have happened in several ways, I admit my choice between these possibilities must be conjectural: but besides the fact that those conjectures become reasons when they are the most probable ones we can infer from the nature of things, and represent the only means we can have for discovering the truth, the conclusions I infer from them will not thus be conjectural, since, on the basis of the principles I have established, another system could not be devised without the

---

[†] constitution *Added 1782.*

same results and from which I could not draw the same conclusions.

This will exempt me from enlarging on my thoughts about the way the passing of time makes up for the improbability of events, or about the surprising effectiveness of very slight causes when they act uninterruptedly; or about the impossibility, on the one hand, of quashing certain hypotheses, and, on the other hand, of giving them the degree of certainty of facts; or about how, when two facts given as real are to be connected by a sequence of intermediary facts that are either unknown or thought to be so, it is for history, when it exists, to produce the facts that connect them; and, when history cannot do this, for philosophy to determine the likely facts that might connect them. Finally, I will be spared from considering how similarity, in reference to events, reduces facts to a much smaller number of different classes than is usually imagined. It is enough for me to present these subjects for the consideration of my critics; it is also enough for me to have set things out in a way that the common reader has no need to consider them at all.

PART II

THE true founder of civil society was the first man who, having enclosed a piece of land, thought of saying, 'This is mine', and came across people simple enough to believe him. How many crimes, wars, murders and how much misery and horror the human race might have been spared if someone had pulled up the stakes or filled in the ditch, and cried out to his fellows: 'Beware of listening to this charlatan. You are lost if you forget that the fruits of the earth belong to all and that the earth itself belongs to no one!' Quite evidently, however, things had by this time reached a point at which they could not continue as they had been, for since the idea of property depends on many anterior ideas that could only have arisen in sequential stages, it was not produced in the human mind all at once. Before arriving at this final stage of the state of nature, men had to make a good deal of progress, acquire considerable ingenuity and knowledge, and transmit and increase them from age to age. So let us go further back into the matter, and try to look from a single viewpoint at the slow chain of events and learning in their most natural order.

Man's first sentiment was that of his existence, and his first concern was that of his own preservation. The products of the earth furnished all the necessary support and prompted him to make use of them by instinct. Hunger and other cravings made him in turn experience various ways of living, but one particular craving goaded him to perpetuate his own species: and this blind inclination, devoid of any sentiment of the heart, occasioned only a purely animal act. Once the need was satisfied, the two sexes no longer recognized each other, and even the child meant nothing to the mother once he could do without her.

Such was the condition of nascent man; such was the life of an animal initially limited to pure sensations, scarcely profiting from the gifts supplied him by nature, much less imagining he could wrest anything from it. Difficulties soon cropped up, however, and man had to learn to overcome them—the height of trees, which prevented him from reaching their fruits; competition from animals seeking to feed on these fruits; the ferocity of animals that were after his life—all this obliged man to engage in physical exercise; he had to make himself agile, fleet of foot, and spirited in combat. He soon found natural weapons at hand, such as stones and tree branches. He learned to surmount nature's obstacles, to battle against other animals if need be, to fight with other men for his subsistence, or to offset what he was forced to cede to the stronger.

As the human race increased, so did its problems. Differences in terrain, soils, climates, and seasons might have forced men to adopt different ways of living. Barren years, long hard winters, and scorching summers that despoiled everything called for a new industriousness. Along the seashores and riverbanks men invented the hook and line, becoming fishermen and eaters of fish. In the forests they made bows and arrows, becoming hunters and warriors. In cold countries they clothed themselves with the hides of the beasts they had slain. Lightning, a volcano, or some happy accident introduced them to fire—a fresh resource against the severity of winter. They learned to preserve this element, then to reproduce it, and eventually to use it to prepare the meats they had once eaten raw.

This repeated use of things different from himself and from each other must naturally have generated in man's mind the perception of certain relations. These relations, which we express by the words 'large', 'small', 'strong', 'weak', 'fast', 'slow', 'fearful', 'bold', and other such ideas, compared when necessary and almost unthinkingly, ultimately produced in him some kind of reflection, or rather a mechanical prudence, that suggested to him the precautions most crucial for his safety.

The new knowledge produced by this development increased his sense of superiority over other animals. He practised setting traps for them; he outsmarted them in a thousand ways, and though several animals surpassed him in strength or fleetness of foot, he in time became the ruler of those who could serve him and the bane of those who could harm him. Thus, his first look at himself triggered his first stirrings of pride; and though hardly yet able to make distinctions of rank, he affirmed the primacy of his species, and so prepared himself far in advance to claim it for himself as an individual.

Although his fellow men were not for him what they are for us and he had little more dealings with them than he had with other animals, they did not go unnoticed. The similarities that he could in time behold between them, his female, and himself, led him to think of those he did not perceive; and, seeing that they all behaved the same way he did in similar circumstances, he concluded that their manner of thinking and feeling was entirely consistent with his own; and once this important truth was well implanted in his mind, he was led to follow, by an intuition as certain as and more immediate than logic, the best rules of conduct he found suitable to observe toward them for his own advantage and safety.

Taught by experience that the lone motive of human action is love of well-being, he was ready to identify the rare circumstances in which the common interest justified his counting on the aid of his fellows, and the even rarer occasions in which competition should make him distrust them. In the former case, he joined them in a flock, or at most in a sort of free association that was binding to no one and lasted only as long as the transient need responsible for it. In the latter case, each person sought his own advantage, either by overt force, if he believed he was strong enough, or by his wits and cunning if he believed he was the weaker.

In this way, men were able gradually to acquire some rough idea of mutual commitments and the benefits of keeping them, but only as much as clear and present interests might require, for men had no foresight, and far from concerning themselves with a distant future, they hardly thought of the next day. When it came to tracking down a deer, everyone realized that he should remain dependably at his post; but if a hare happened to pass within reach of one of them, he undoubtedly would not have hesitated to run off after it and, after catching his prey, he would have troubled himself little about causing his companions to lose theirs.

It is easy to see that such dealings among them would not require a language any more sophisticated than that of crows or monkeys, which band together in much the same way. The universal human language must long have been made up of inarticulate cries, numerous gestures, and some imitative noises, to which men in each region, by adding a few articulated and conventional sounds (the establishment of which is, as I have already said, none too easy to explain), arrived at particular, though crude and imperfect, languages, rather like those we still find today among various savage nations. I proceed in a flash across many centuries, forced by the passage of time, the profusion of the things I have to say, and the almost imperceptible progress of the beginnings of things—for the more slowly the events unfolded, the more rapidly they may be described.

These first slow developments eventually enabled men to make more rapid ones. The more discerning the mind became, the more industrious men became. Soon, ceasing to doze under the first tree or to withdraw into caves, men found various sorts of hard sharp stones to serve as hatchets for cutting wood, tilling the soil, and constructing huts out of branches, which they then thought of overlaying with clay and mud. This was the age of a first revolution in which families were established and differentiated, property of a sort introduced, and hence perhaps even then many quarrels and fights first arose. Nevertheless, because the strongest men were likely the first to build huts that they felt capable of defending, the weak likely found it quicker and safer to imitate them rather than try to oust them, and, as for those who already had huts, no one tried to seize his neighbour's, less because he did not own it than because it was pointless to do so and he could not take it over without exposing himself to an energetic set-to with the family who inhabited it.

The first stirrings of the heart issued from this new situation, which brought together husbands and wives, fathers and children, in a common dwelling; the habit of living side by side occasioned the sweetest of human sentiments: conjugal and paternal love. Every family became a small society, all the more united because its only bonds were freedom and mutual affection; it was also at this time that the first differences were established in the ways of living of the two sexes, which had hitherto had but one. The women started staying more at home and grew used to tending the hut and the children while the men went off in pursuit of their common subsistence. The two sexes started living a gentler life, losing some of their ferocity and vigour, but though each one became less fit individually to contend with wild beasts, it was easier, on the other hand, to cluster together to resist them jointly.

In this new state, with its simple and solitary life, with few needs and very few tools invented to meet them, men enjoyed a good deal of leisure and used it to procure for themselves many conveniences unknown to their forefathers; and this was the first yoke they unwittingly imposed on themselves and the first source of the evils they were preparing for their descendants. For not only did these men proceed to lull both body and mind; through habitual use these conveniences also lost almost all their pleasurableness, degenerating into genuine needs, and the deprivation of them became much more painful than the possession of them was pleasing; and people were unhappy in losing them without being happy in possessing them.

Here we can see somewhat more clearly how the use of speech was gradually established and improved within the family, and we can further speculate as to how particular causes could have made language spread and hastened its progress by making it more necessary. Great floods or earthquakes surrounded inhabited regions with seas or precipices; upheavals on the globe caused portions of the continent to break off into islands. We can suppose that among men thus brought together and forced to live in each other's company, a common tongue must have developed earlier than among those who still wandered freely through the forests of the mainland. Thus it is distinctly possible that we owe the use of speech to islanders who brought it to us following their first attempts at navigation, and it is at least highly probable that society and languages were born on islands and perfected there before they were known on the continent.

Everything begins to take on a new appearance. Men who had once roamed the woods, having taken up a fixed location, slowly came together, gathered in various clusters, and in each region eventually formed a particular nation, united by customs and character—not by rules and laws, but through having a common way of living and eating and through the common influence of the same climate. Ultimately, constant proximity could not fail to beget some relations between different families. Young people of opposite sexes lived in neighbouring huts; and the transient intercourse demanded by nature soon leads, through time spent in each other's company, to another intercourse that is just as sweet but more permanent. People become accustomed to judging various objects and making comparisons; they gradually acquire ideas of value and beauty, which in turn yield preferences. From seeing each other, people cannot do without seeing each other even more. A tender and sweet sentiment steals into their souls and, at the least opposition, becomes a raging fury; jealousy awakens with love; discord triumphs, and the sweetest of passions receives the sacrifice of human blood.

As ideas and feelings succeeded one another, and hearts and minds were cultivated, the human race became more sociable, contacts increased, and bonds grew tighter. People developed the habit of gathering together in front of their huts or around a large tree; song and dance, true children of love and leisure, became the entertainment, or rather the occupation, of the idle men and women thus flocked together. Each person began to gaze on the others and to want to be gazed upon himself, and what came to be prized was public esteem. Anyone who best sang or danced; he who was the most handsome, the strongest, the most skilful, or the most eloquent came to be the most highly regarded, and this was the first step toward inequality and also toward vice. These first preferences gave rise, on the one side, to vanity and scorn, and on the other, to shame and envy; and the ferment produced by these new leavens eventually led to concoctions ruinous to happiness and innocence.

Once men learned to appraise one another and formed the idea of esteem, everyone claimed a right to it, and no one could then be denied it without taking affront. This was the source of the first duties of courtesy, even among savages; and henceforth every intentional wrong became a grave offence, for along with the harm resulting from the affront, the offended party often saw an insult to his person as more intolerable than the harm itself. Thus, because the attack of one person scorned by another was commensurate with the value he placed on himself, revenge became terrible, and men bloodthirsty and cruel. This is precisely the stage reached by most of the savage peoples known to us, and because so many writers have not sufficiently distinguished between ideas and seen how far those peoples already are from the first state of nature, these thinkers have hastened to conclude that man is naturally cruel and needs civil government to make him gentler, although in truth nothing is gentler than man in his primitive state where, placed by nature midway between the stupidity of brutes and the fatal enlightenment of civilized man and limited equally by reason and instinct to ward off the evils threatening him, his natural pity deters him from doing harm to anyone, even when he has encountered harm himself. For according to the wise Locke: 'Where there is no property, there is no injury.'*

It should be noted, however, that once society came into existence and relations between individuals were established, different traits of men were required from those they owed to their primitive constitution; that since morality began to be introduced into human actions and since prior to the existence of laws each man was the sole judge and avenger of the offenses committed against him, the goodness suitable to the pure state of nature was no longer suitable to the nascent society; that punishments had to be more severe as the occasions for giving offense became more common and the terror of revenge had to stand in for the check of laws. Thus, although men had come to be less patient and their natural pity had been somewhat attenuated, this period in the development of human faculties, striking a good balance between the indolence of the primitive state and the fervid activity of our own vanity, must have been the happiest and most enduring age. The more we reflect on it, the more we realize that this state was the best for man and the least subject to revolutions; (P) and that man can have left it only as the result of some fatal accident that, for the common good, ought never to have happened. The example of savages, almost always found to be at this stage, appears to confirm that the human race was made to remain there forever, that this state was the true youth of the world, and that all subsequent advances appear to be so many steps toward improvement of the individual but, in fact, toward the enfeeblement of the species.

As long as men were content with their rustic huts, as long as they confined themselves to stitching their garments of hides with thorns or fishbones, and adorning themselves with feathers or shells, to painting their bodies with various colours, to improving or decorating their bows and arrows, and to carving fishing-boats or a few crude musical instruments; in short, so long as they applied themselves only to work that one person alone could accomplish and to arts that did not require the collaboration of several hands, they lived as free, healthy, good, and happy lives as their nature permitted and continued to enjoy among themselves the delights of independent activity. But from the moment one man needed help from another, and as soon as they found it useful for one man to have provisions enough for two, equality evaporated, property was introduced, and work became mandatory; vast forests were transformed into sunny open country that had to be watered with the sweat of man, and where slavery and adversity were soon seen to germinate and ripen with the crops.

This great revolution followed from the invention of the arts of agriculture and metallurgy. For the poet it is gold and silver, but for the philosopher it is iron and wheat that first civilized and ruined the human race. Neither of these arts were known to the savages of America who thus have remained savages; the other peoples seem to have remained

barbarians as long as they practised one of these arts and not
the other, and one of the best reasons why Europe, if not the
earliest to be civilized, has been at least more continuously
and better civilized than other parts of the world, may be
that it is the richest in iron and the most productive of
wheat.

It is very difficult to envision how men came first to know
and use iron, for it is unlikely they would think on their own
of drawing ore from the mine and giving it the needed
preparations for smelting before knowing what the results
would be. On the other hand, we can even less readily credit
this discovery to some accidental fire, for mines are formed
only in dry areas devoid of trees and plants, so one might say
that nature had taken pains to hide this fatal secret from us.
Hence there remains only the phenomenal event of some
volcano disgorging molten metallic substances and thereby
giving those who witnessed it the idea of duplicating this
natural process. We would also have to assume those men
had enough drive to undertake such onerous labour and
enough foresight to project far into the future the benefits
they might derive from it, which is scarcely creditable even to
minds more developed than theirs.

As for agriculture, its principle was known long before the
practice of it was launched, and it is indeed highly unlikely
that men who perpetually lived off trees and plants would
not rather quickly get an idea of the means nature uses
to reproduce vegetation. But men's activity probably took
that turn only very late—because trees, which together with
hunting and fishing supplied their food, needed no care, or
because men had no knowledge of the use of wheat or no
tools for farming it, or because of lack of foresight concerning future needs, or because of a lack of a way to prevent
others from seizing the fruits of their labour. As men became
more skilled, we can believe that they began using sharp
stones and pointed sticks to grow a few vegetables or roots
around their huts; although it took a long time before they
knew how to process wheat or had the tools needed for
large-scale growing; they also had to learn that in order to
devote oneself to this activity and sow the land, one must

accept an initial loss for the sake of a greater gain in the future—a prescience quite alien to the savage's turn of mind since, as I have said, he is hard pressed to imagine in the morning the needs he will have that evening.

The invention of the other arts must thus have been necessary to compel the human race to take up agriculture. When some men were needed to smelt and forge iron, others were needed to supply them with food. The more the number of labourers grew, the fewer hands were engaged in providing for the common subsistence, without there being any fewer mouths to consume it; and because some men needed foodstuffs in return for their iron, others finally discovered the secret of using iron to increase the supply of food. From this arose, on the one hand, plowing and agriculture, and, on the other, the art of working metals and extending their uses.

The cultivation of the land necessarily led to its division, and the recognition of property led to the first rules of justice: for in order to render to each his own,* each must be able to own something; moreover, as men began to direct their gaze into the future and all saw that they had some goods to lose, there was no one who did not fear reprisals against himself for the wrongs he might do to others. This origin is all the more natural because the idea of property could not conceivably have arisen from anything other than manual labour, for it is not apparent what else besides his own labour* a man can add to things he has not made, in order to make them his property. Labour alone gives the grower the right to the crops from the land he has tilled and this consequently gives him the right to the produce of the land and hence to the land itself, at least until the harvest, and hence from year to year, that which constitutes uninterrupted possession is easily transformed into property. Grotius* says that when the ancients gave Ceres the title of Legislatrix, and the name Thesmaphoria to the festival celebrated in her honour, they implied that the division of land had produced a new sort of right, that is, the right to property, which is different from the right derived from natural law.

Things in this state might have remained equal if abilities had been equal and if, for example, the use of iron and the consumption of foodstuffs had always exactly matched each other; because, however, this equilibrium was protected by nothing, it was soon upset: the stronger produced more work, the more skilled did better work, and the cleverer found ways to shorten their labour. The farmer had greater need of iron or the blacksmith greater need of wheat and, with both working the same amount, the one earned a great deal while the other had scarcely enough to live on. Thus, natural inequality gradually leads to inequality of rank, and the differences between men, augmented by differences of circumstance, become more conspicuous and lasting in their effects and begin to exert a correspondingly powerful influence over the fate of individuals.

Once things reached this point, we can readily imagine the rest. I shall not dwell on a description of the successive invention of the other arts, the development of languages, the testing and use of abilities, the inequality of fortunes, the use and misuse of wealth, and all the consequent details that can easily be given by any of us. I shall simply confine myself to casting a glance over the human race as it fitted into this new order of things.

Behold, then, all our faculties trained, our memory and imagination in play, our pride engaged, our reason activated, and our minds as near-perfect as possible. Behold all the natural characteristics called into action, every man's rank and fate settled, not only as to the amount of his possessions and power to help or to harm, but also as to his intelligence, good looks, strength or skill, merit or abilities; and because only these traits could elicit esteem, it soon became necessary to have them or purport to have them. It was soon to one's advantage to be other than one actually was. Being and appearing became two quite different things, and from this distinction emerged striking ostentation, deceitful cunning, and all the vices that follow in their wake. From another point of view, behold man, once free and independent, now subject, so to speak, through a multitude of new needs, to all of nature and above all to his fellow men, whose slave he has in a sense become, even when he becomes their master. For if he is rich, he needs their services; if he is poor he needs their aid; and even a position in between does not enable him to do without them. Thus, he must constantly seek to involve others in his lot, and get them to see an advantage, either real or apparent, in working for his benefit: all of which makes him deceitful and crafty with some people, harsh and domineering with others, and forces him to hoodwink all those he needs if he cannot make them fear him and when he does not consider it to his advantage to be of service to them. Finally, in all men a consuming ambition, the burning passion to increase one's relative fortune, less out of real need than to make oneself superior to others, inspires a dark propensity to harm each other, a secret jealousy that is all the more dangerous because, to strike out from a more secure position, it often assumes the mask of benevolence; in short, we have competition and rivalry on the one hand, and antagonistic interests on the other, and always the hidden desire to gain some advantage at other people's expense. All these evils are the first effects of property and the inseparable escort of nascent inequality.

Before the invention of symbols to represent it, wealth could hardly consist of anything except land and livestock, the only real goods that men could possess. When, however, inheritances so increased in number and extent that they covered all the land and every estate bordered on another one, none could be enlarged except at the expense of some neighbouring one, and the landless supernumeraries whom frailty or indolence barred from acquiring anything for themselves, became poor without having lost anything, because, with everything changing around them, they alone remained unchanged and so were obliged to receive—or steal—their subsistence from the hands of the rich. Out of this situation arose either domination and servitude, or plunder and violence, depending on the different characters of the rich and the poor. The rich, for their part, had hardly learned the joys of domination before they disdained all other ones, and using their current slaves to subdue new ones, they dreamed only of subjugating and enslaving their neighbours, like those ravenous wolves that, having once tasted human flesh, reject all other nourishment and thenceforth desire only to feed on man.

Thus, with the mightiest or the poorest regarding their powers or their needs as a kind of right to the belongings of others, equivalent, according to them, to the right of property, the loss of equality was succeeded by the most appalling disorder. Thus, the encroachments of the rich, the thievery of the poor, and the unbridled passions of everyone, stifling natural pity and the still-hushed voice of justice, made men greedy, ambitious, and wicked. Between the right of the strongest and the right of the first occupant there arose a perpetual conflict that ended only in fights and murders. (Q) Nascent society made way for the most horrible state of war: the human race, degraded and ravaged, could not then retrace its path or renounce its unfortunate acquisitions, but working only toward its shame through the misuse of faculties that should be its honour, brought itself to the brink of ruin.

> Attonitus novitate mali, divesque miserque,
> Effugere optat opes, et quae modo voverat, odit.*

It was at last impossible for men not to devote some thought to this awful situation and the calamities that had befallen them. The rich in particular must have realized the great disadvantages to them of a perpetual war in which they bore all the costs and in which the risk of life was universal but the risk of property theirs alone. Furthermore, whatever disguise they might put upon their usurpations, they were well aware that these were based solely on precarious and sham rights, and that force could divest them of what force alone had procured and they would thus have no grounds for complaint. Even those who had been enriched by their own industry could not base their right to their property on better credentials. They might well have said: 'I built this wall; I earned the right to this field by my own labour.' They might be answered with 'Who gave you the boundary lines? And on what basis do you demand payment from us for work we never requested of you? Are you unaware that vast numbers of your fellow men suffer or perish from need of the things that you have to excess, and that you required the explicit and unanimous consent of the whole human race for you to appropriate from the common subsistence anything besides that required for your own?' Lacking valid reasons to justify himself and sufficient strength to defend himself; handily overpowering an individual but overpowered himself by bandits; alone against all and, owing to mutual jealousies, unable to form alliances with his peers against enemies banded together in the shared hope of plunder, the rich man, goaded by necessity, eventually conceived of the shrewdest scheme ever to enter the human mind: to employ on his behalf the very forces of his attackers, to make his opponents his defenders, to inspire them with new slogans, and give them new institutions as favourable to him as natural right was detrimental.

To this end, after showing his neighbours the horror of a situation that pitted all against the others, made their possessions as burdensome as their needs, and that yielded no safety to those in poverty or in prosperity, he readily concocted specious reasons to guide men to his goal. 'Let us unite' he said to them, 'to protect the weak from oppression, hold the overdesirous in check, and ensure for each the possession of what belongs to him. Let us establish rules of justice and peace that everyone is obligated to conform to without favouring any one person, and that will make amends, as it were, for the caprices of fortune by subjecting the powerful and the weak equally to reciprocal duties. In short, rather than train our forces against each other, let us unite them together in one supreme power that will govern us all according to wise laws, protect and defend all the members of the association, fend off common enemies, and preserve us in everlasting concord.'

Much less than the equivalent of this speech was needed to win over men so uncultivated and gullible, especially as they had too many scores to settle among themselves to do without arbiters, and too much greed and ambition to do for long without masters. All ran headlong for their chains in the belief that they were securing their liberty; for although they had enough reason to see the advantages of political institutions, they did not have enough experience to foresee their dangers. Those most capable of predicting the abuses were precisely the ones who counted on profiting from them; and the wise ones saw that men must resolve to sacrifice one part of their freedom in order to preserve the other, just as a wounded man has his arm cut off to save the rest of his body.

Such was, or must have been, the origin of society and of laws, which put new shackles on the weak and gave new powers to the rich, (R) which destroyed natural freedom irretrievably, laid down for all time the law of property and inequality, made clever usurpation into an irrevocable right, and henceforth subjected, for the benefit of a few ambitious men, the human race to labour, servitude, and misery. We can easily see how the founding of one society made that of all the rest inevitable, and how, in order to hold their own against united forces, others in turn had to unite. Societies, as they proliferated and spread, soon covered the whole surface of the earth, and it was no longer possible to find a single corner on the globe where one might free oneself from the yoke and shield one's head from the often precariously held sword that every man saw perpetually dangling over him. Because civil law thus became the common rule over citizens, the law of nature obtained only between the various societies where, under the name of law of nations, it was moderated by certain tacit conventions designed to allow for relations and to stand in for the natural commiseration that, from society to society, having lost nearly all the force it had from man to man, lives on only in a few great cosmopolitan souls, who break through the imaginary barriers between peoples and, following the example of their sovereign creator, include the whole human race in their benevolence.

The bodies politic, thus remaining in the state of nature in relation to each other, soon experienced the same disadvantages that had forced individuals to leave it; the state of nature proved even more catastrophic to these large bodies than it had once been for the individuals of whom they were composed. From this there arose wars between nations, battles, killings, reprisals that make nature shudder and offend reason, and all those horrible preconceived ideas that make a virtue out of the shedding of human blood. Perfectly decent men learned to count among their duties the killing of their fellows; and in time men came to massacre one another by the thousands without knowing why, committing more murders in a single day's battle and more atrocities in a single city's capture than had been committed in the state of nature for whole centuries over the entire face of the earth. Such are the first observed effects of the division of the human race into different societies. But let us return to their beginnings.

I know that many have suggested other origins for political societies, such as conquest by the most powerful or the union of the weak, but the choice between these causes is immaterial to what I wish to establish. The one I have just sketched, however, seems to me the most natural for the following reasons: (1) Because in the first place, the right of conquest is not a right at all and so could not have been the basis of any other; the conqueror and the people conquered will always remain in a state of war toward each other, unless the conquered nation, with its freedom fully restored, voluntarily chooses its conqueror for its ruler. Up to that point, whatever capitulations were made were based solely on violence and are thereby invalid, so there cannot on this hypothesis be any authentic society or body politic or any law but the law of the strongest. (2) Because in the latter case, the words 'strong' and 'weak' are equivocal; for during the period between the establishment of the right to property or the right of the first occupant and the establishment of political governments, the meaning of these terms is better expressed by the words 'poor' and 'rich,' since before the introduction of laws a man's only means of subjugating his peers was to raid their goods or make them a part of his own. (3) Because, with nothing to lose but their freedom, it would have been an act of lunacy for the poor voluntarily to divest themselves of the only good that still remained to them and get nothing in return. It was much easier, however, to harm the rich, who were vulnerable, so to speak, in every part of their wealth and thus had to take more steps for their own protection; and lastly it is reasonable to believe that a thing was invented by those to whom it was advantageous rather than by those to whom it was detrimental.

The nascent government had no durable and regular form. The lack of experience and wisdom made only current troubles salient, and men thought of remedies for other ills only when they became clearly evident. Despite the efforts of the wisest legislators, the political state remained ever flawed, because it was almost entirely the handiwork of chance, and, because this state got off to a poor start, time, though revealing defects and suggesting remedies, could never repair the defects of the constitution. Constitutions were constantly patched up, even though it was really necessary to begin by clearing the ground and scrapping the old materials, as Lycurgus did in Sparta, in order to build a solid edifice. At first, society consisted only of a few general conventions which all individuals committed themselves to observe and which the community guaranteed for each one of them. Experience was bound to expose the weakness of such a constitution and the ease with which offenders could escape conviction or punishment for crimes of which only the public was witness and judge. The laws were bound to be circumvented in a thousand ways; troubles and disorders were ever bound to multiply until men at last thought of handing over the dangerous trust of public authority to certain individuals and assigning to magistrates the task of securing compliance to the deliberations of the people, for to say that the leaders were chosen before the confederation was created, and that ministers responsible for the laws existed before the laws themselves is a suggestion unworthy of serious debate.

It would be no more reasonable to believe that men first flung themselves unconditionally and irrevocably into the arms of an absolute master, and that the first means that occurred to proud and spirited men for providing for their common security was to rush headlong into slavery. Indeed, why did they give themselves overseers if not as a defence against oppression, and a means of safeguarding their possessions, their freedoms, and their lives, which are, so to speak, the constitutive elements of their being? Since the worst thing that can happen to someone in the relations between one man and another is to find oneself at the other's mercy, would it not be contrary to common sense to hand over to a superior the only things one needs his help to preserve? What thing of equivalent value could he offer them in return for the surrender of so precious a right? And if he had dared to demand this surrender on the pretext of defending them, would he not promptly have been given the answer from the fable:* 'What more will the enemy do to us?' Thus, it is undeniable—and indeed the fundamental principle of all political right—that people have instituted leaders in order to defend their freedom and not to enslave themselves. 'If we have a prince', said Pliny to Trajan, 'it is in order that he may preserve us from having a master.'*

Politicians* repeat the same sophistries about the love of freedom as do philosophers about the state of nature; on the strength of things that they see, they make judgements about very different things that they have not seen, and they attribute to men a natural inclination for servitude because of the patience with which the slaves they see before them endure theirs, failing to remember that freedom is like innocence and virtue: one appreciates its value only as long as one possesses it, and, when one loses it, the taste for it is [also] lost. 'I know the delights of your country,' said Brasidas to a satrap, who was comparing the life of Sparta with that of Persepolis, 'but you cannot know the pleasures of mine.'*

Just as an unbroken horse tosses its mane, stamps the ground with its hoof, and rears up furiously at the mere approach of the bit, while a broken-in horse patiently suffers even the whip and spurs, savage man will not bend his neck to the yoke that civilized man wears without a whimper; savage man prefers the most tempestuous freedom to the most tranquil subservience. Hence it is not to the degradation of enslaved peoples that we should look in judging man's natural disposition toward or against servitude, but rather to the wonders worked by all free peoples in saving themselves from oppression. I know that enslaved peoples do nothing but boast of the peace and repose they enjoy in their chains, and that *miserrimam servitutem pacem appellant.** When, however, I see free peoples sacrificing pleasure, repose, wealth, power, and even life itself for the sake of preserving the lone good that is so scorned by those who have lost it; when I see animals, born free and abhorring captivity, smashing their heads against the bars of their prison; when I see multitudes of naked savages scorn European pleasures and brave hunger, fire, the sword, and death just to safeguard their independence, I feel that it is not for slaves to deliberate about freedom.

As for paternal authority, from which several writers have derived absolute government and all society, it is enough, without referring to the refutations of Locke and Sidney,* to notice that nothing on earth could be further from the brutal spirit of despotism than the gentleness of the authority that looks more to the advantage of him who obeys than to the self-interest of him who commands; and to notice that, according to the law of nature, the father is the child's master only as long as his help is needed and that beyond this point the two are equals, the son becoming perfectly independent of his father and owing his elder only respect and not obedience, for gratitude is clearly a duty to be owed and not a right to be demanded. Instead of saying that civil society derives from paternal power, we ought to say, on the contrary, that paternal power derives its main force from society: no individual was recognized as the father of several children until they lived together with him. The goods of the father, of which he is truly the master, are the ties that keep his children dependent on him, and he may choose to give them a share of his estate if they have earned it through regular deference to his wishes. The subjects of a despot, however, are far from having some similar favour to expect of him, because since they are his exclusive possession—they and all they have belong to him as his personal property, or at least so he claims—they are reduced to receiving from him

as a favour whatever he leaves them of their own belongings.
He dispenses justice when he robs them; and grace when he
allows them to live.

To continue to examine facts in the light of right, we find
no more substance than truth in the so-called voluntary
establishment of tyranny, and it would be difficult to prove
the validity of a contract that was binding on only one of the
parties, that gave everything to one party and nothing to
the other, and that could be changed only to the detriment
of the one who commits himself. Even today, this odious
system is quite unlike that of good and wise monarchs,
especially of the kings of France, as can be seen from several
statements in their edicts and particularly in the following
passage from a famous document published in 1667 in the
name, and by the order, of Louis XIV:

Let it not therefore be said that the sovereign is not subject to the
laws of his state since the contrary proposition is a truth of the law
of nations, which flattery has sometimes denied but which true
princes have defended as a tutelary divinity of their states. How
much more legitimate is it to say with the wise Plato that the perfect
felicity of a kingdom is for a prince to be obeyed by his subjects, for
the prince to obey the law, and for the law to be just and always
directed to the public good.*

I shall not dwell on whether, since freedom is the noblest
of man's faculties, we degrade our nature by lowering ourselves to the level of beasts enslaved by instinct, and even
to offend the Author of our being by renouncing unconditionally the most precious of all his gifts and commit all
the crimes he has forbidden in order to appease a cruel or
unreasonable overseer, nor whether that sublime craftsman
would be angrier at seeing his finest handiwork destroyed
than at seeing it dishonoured.† I shall merely ask by what
right those who are unafraid to degrade themselves to this

---

† I shall disregard, if you will, the authority of Barbeyrac, who follows
Locke in flatly asserting that no one can sell his freedom to the extent of
submitting himself to an arbitrary power that may use him as it fancies. 'For
that,' he adds, 'would be to sell one's own life, of which one is not the
master.'* *Added 1782.*

point could subject their descendants to the same ignominy, and on behalf of their posterity renounce things that were not derived from their generosity and without which life itself is a burden to all who are worthy of it?

Pufendorf says that just as one can transfer one's goods to others by agreements and contracts, one can also divest oneself of one's freedom in someone else's favour.* This seems to me a very bad argument, for, first of all, the goods I give up become something utterly separate from me, and I am indifferent to any mistreatment of them, but it is crucial to me that my freedom not be mistreated, and I cannot lay myself open to becoming an instrument of crime without incurring the guilt for whatever crime I am forced to commit. Furthermore, because the right to property is only a matter of convention and human institution, everyone may dispose of his belongings as he pleases; but it is not the same with the essential gifts of nature, such as life and freedom, which everyone is allowed to enjoy and of which it is at least doubtful whether anyone has the right to divest himself. By giving up freedom, a man debases his being: by giving up life, he annihilates it in so far as he can, and since no worldly goods could compensate for the loss of either life or freedom, renouncing them at any price at all would be an offence against both nature and reason. Even if one could give up one's freedom like one's belongings, however, the difference would be very great for one's children, who enjoy their father's goods only by the handing down of his right to them, whereas, because freedom is a gift they get from nature for being human, their parents never had a right to deprive them of it. Thus, just as it was necessary to do violence to nature to establish slavery, nature had to be altered to maintain this right, and the jurists who have solemnly declared that the child of a slave would be born a slave have, in other words, decided that a man will not be born a man.

It thus seems to me certain that governments did not originate in arbitrary power, which is only the endpoint in the corruption of governments, one that eventually brings them back to the very law of the strongest that they were first introduced to remedy; but even if they did begin this way, such power is inherently illegitimate and hence could not serve as the basis for rights in society nor, hence, for the established inequality in society.

Without entering here into a study that has yet to be done on the nature of the fundamental pact underlying all government,* I shall confine myself to follow common opinion by considering the establishment of the body politic as a true contract between a people and the leaders they choose, a contract by which both parties commit themselves to observe the laws that are spelled out in its articles and that form the bonds of their union. Because the people have, with respect to social relations, combined all their wills into a single one, all the articles by which that will is expressed become fundamental laws that obligate every member of the state without exception; and one of these laws regulates the choice and powers of the magistrates assigned to oversee the execution of the others. This power extends to everything that can uphold the constitution without going so far as to change it. Added to this are the honours that make the laws and their ministers worthy of respect, and prerogatives that personally reimburse the ministers for the hard work involved in good administration. The magistrate, for his part, pledges to use the power entrusted to him only in accordance with the intentions of his constituents, to uphold each person in the peaceful enjoyment of what belongs to him, and at all times to prefer the public interest to his own advantage.

Before experience showed, or knowledge of the human heart made men foresee, the inevitable abuses of such a constitution, it must have seemed all the better because those assigned to ensure its preservation were those who had the greatest stake in it. For since the magistrature and its rights were established solely upon the fundamental laws, as soon as the laws were destroyed, the magistrates would lose their legitimacy; the people would no longer owe them obedience; and because the essence of the state was not the magistrate but the law, each person would by right revert to his natural freedom.

If we think about it attentively, we could find new reasons to confirm this point and to see from the very nature of the contract that it cannot be irrevocable, for if there were no superior power able to ensure the adherence of the contracting parties, or to compel them to fulfil their reciprocal commitments, each party would remain the sole judge of his own cause, and each would always have the right to repudiate the contract whenever he considered that the other had violated its conditions, or whenever those conditions ceased to suit him. It would appear that this principle could serve as a basis for the right of abdication. Considering, as we do here, things established by man, if the magistrate, who holds all the power and appropriates for himself all the advantages of the contract, none the less enjoys the right to relinquish his authority, the people, who pay for all their leaders' mistakes, ought all the more to have the right to disavow their dependence. But the shocking dissensions and endless disorders that this dangerous power would necessarily occasion show us better than anything else how much human governments needed a basis more solid than reason alone, and how necessary it was for public tranquillity that the divine will should intervene to give the sovereign authority a sacred and inviolable character that deprived the subjects of the fatal right of giving it away. If religion had given only this benefit to men, that would be enough to oblige them all to adopt and cherish religion, despite its abuses, for it prevents even more bloodshed than that caused by fanaticism. But let us follow the thread of our hypothesis.

The various forms of government originate in the greater or lesser differences existing between individuals at the time the government is established. If one man was pre-eminent in power, virtue, wealth, or ability to inspire confidence, he alone was elected magistrate, and the state became monarchical. If several men, more or less equal among themselves, prevailed over all others, they were elected conjointly and made up an aristocracy. Those whose fortunes and abilities were less disparate, and who were less far removed from the state of nature, kept the supreme administration in common and formed a democracy. Time has confirmed which of these forms was the most advantageous for men. Some remained subject to laws alone; others soon obeyed masters. Citizens wished to keep their liberty; subjects thought only of taking it away from their neighbours, finding unbearable the prospect of others enjoying a good they no longer enjoyed themselves. In short, on one side were riches and conquests; on the other, happiness and virtue.

In these various governments, all magistratures were originally elective; and where wealth did not carry the day, preference was accorded to merit, which produces a natural authority, and to age, which offers experience in business and self-possession in deliberations. The elders of the Hebrews, the gerontes of Sparta, the Senate of Rome, and the very etymology of our word *seigneur*, show how greatly old age was once respected. The more often elections went to men of advanced age, however, the more frequently they had to be held, and the more muddles resulted; intrigues sprang up, factions formed, parties became acrimonious, civil wars broke out, and eventually the blood of citizens was sacrificed for the supposed well-being of the state, and men were on the verge of lapsing into the anarchy of earlier times. Ambitious leaders took advantage of this situation to set up sinecures in their own families; the people, already accustomed to dependence, tranquillity, and the comforts of life, and incapable of breaking their chains, consented to an increase in their servitude for the purpose of securing their tranquillity. Thus, the leaders, having become hereditary, accustomed themselves to looking on their magistratures as family property, to regarding themselves as the owners of a state in which they were originally only the officers, to calling their fellow citizens their slaves, to counting them, like cattle, among their belongings, and to calling themselves the equals of the gods and the kings of kings.*

As we trace the march of inequality in these various revolutions, we find that the establishment of law and the right of property was the first stage, the institution of the magistrature the second, and the transformation of legitimate into arbitrary power the third and last. Thus, the status of rich and poor was sanctioned in the first age, that of strong and weak in the second, and in the third that of master and slave, the ultimate degree of inequality to which all the others at last lead until new revolutions dissolve the government altogether or bring it closer to legitimacy.

To see the necessity of this progression, we should consider less the reasons for establishing the body politic than the form this body's actions takes and the disadvantages it then involves, for the wrongs that make social institutions necessary are the same as those that make the abuse of those institutions inevitable. Because—leaving aside the special case of Sparta, where the laws dealt chiefly with the education of children and the customs Lycurgus so well established made additional laws almost superfluous—laws, which are generally weaker than the passions, curb men without changing them, it is easily proven that any government that, without being corrupted or degenerate, always worked in exact accord with the purposes of its establishment, would have been instituted unnecessarily, and that a country in which no one operated outside the law or manipulated the magistracy would need neither laws nor magistrates.

Political distinctions necessarily lead to civil distinctions. The growing inequality between the people and their leaders is soon manifest among individuals, and is modified in them in a thousand ways depending on passions, abilities and circumstances. The magistrate cannot usurp illegitimate power without finding operatives to whom he is forced to yield some part of it. Furthermore, citizens allow themselves to be oppressed only so far as they are impelled by blind ambition; and fixing their eyes below rather than above themselves, they relish domination more than independence, and agree to wear chains for the sake of in turn imposing chains on others. It is difficult to reduce to obedience a man who has no wish to command, and the most crafty politician could not succeed in subjugating men whose only wish was to be free; inequality, however, readily spreads to craven and ambitious souls, ever ready to run the risks of fortune and almost indifferent about whether they command or obey, depending on which is more advantageous to them. Thus the time must have come when the eyes of the people were so bedazzled that their leaders had only to say to the least of men: 'Be great, with all your posterity,' and that man forthwith appeared great in everyone's eyes as well as in his own, and his descendants were exalted in proportion to their distance from him; the more remote and uncertain the cause, the greater the effect; the more idlers who could be counted in a family, the more illustrious it became.

If this were the place to go into details, I could easily explain how[†] inequality of influence and authority becomes inevitable among individuals (S) as soon as, united in the same society, they are forced to compare themselves to one another and take account of the differences they find in their constant dealings with one another. These differences are of several kinds, but because wealth, nobility or rank, power, and personal merit are generally the four chief attributes by which one is judged in society, I would argue that the harmony or conflict between these various forces is the surest indication of whether the state is well or badly constituted. I would show that of these four kinds of inequality, personal qualities are the source of all the others and wealth the last of them to which they can all be reduced in the end, for since wealth is the most immediately useful to well-being and the easiest to transmit, it can readily be used to buy all the rest—an observation that enables us to make a fairly exact assessment of how far each people has come from its original institution and the progress it has made toward the extreme limit of corruption. I would observe how this universal desire for reputation, honours, and privilege, which consumes us all, exercises and compares our abilities and strengths; I would show how it excites and multiplies passions, and how, in making all men competitors, rivals, or rather enemies, it causes every day failures and successes and catastrophes of every kind by having so many aspirants compete in the same contest; I would show that this burning desire to be talked about, this greed for distinction that keeps us ever in turmoil is responsible for what is best and what is worst among men, for our virtues and our vices, for our sciences and our errors, for our conquerors and our philosophers—that is, for a host of bad things as compared to a few good ones. Lastly, I

[†] even without the involvement of government   *Added 1782.*

would prove that if one sees a handful of powerful and rich men at the pinnacle of opulence and fortune, while the crowd below grovels in obscurity and wretchedness, it is because the former valued the things they enjoy only because others are deprived of them, and even without changing their condition, they would cease to rejoice if the people ceased to suffer.

These details alone, however, would provide material for a substantial volume that weighed the advantages and disadvantages of any government in relation to the rights of the state of nature, and that would unmask all the various faces behind which inequality has appeared up to the present and perhaps in future centuries, according to the nature of governments and the revolutions time will inevitably bring about. We would see the multitude oppressed from within as a consequence of the very precautions taken against external threats; we would see a constant increase in oppression without the oppressed ever being in a position to know where it would end, or what legitimate means they had for halting it. We would see the rights of citizens and the freedom of nations gradually extinguished, and the protests of the weak treated as the mutterings of sedition. We would see politics restrict the honour of defending the common cause to a venal segment of the populace; we would consequently see the necessity of taxation arise and the disheartened farmer quitting his fields even in peacetime, and forsaking his plough to gird on the sword. We would see bizarre and deadly codes of honour arise. Sooner or later, we would see the homeland's defenders become the enemy, forever holding a dagger over their fellow citizens, soldiers who in time would be heard to say to their country's oppressor:

> Pectore si fratris gladium juguloque parentis
> Condere me jubeas, gravidaeque in viscera partu
> Conjugis, invita peragam tamen omnia dextra.*

From the extreme inequality of conditions and fortunes, from the diversity of passions and talents, from useless or pernicious arts, and silly sciences would arise hosts of preconceived ideas, all contrary to reason, happiness, and virtue; we would see leaders stirring up everything that might weaken assemblies of men by disuniting them, everything that might give society an air of seeming concord and sow in it the seeds of real disunity, everything that might inspire distrust and mutual hatred in different social orders through conflict between their rights and their interests, and by these means strengthen the power that curbs them all.

From the midst of this disorder and these revolutions, despotism, gradually rearing its ugly head and swallowing up everything that it had seen to be good and sound in all parts of the state, would in the end manage to trample underfoot the people as well as the laws and establish itself upon the ruins of the republic. The times leading to this final change would be times of trouble and calamities; but eventually all would be devoured by the monster, and the people would cease to have leaders and laws, only tyrants. Nor, from this moment on, would there be any morality or virtues, for wherever it reigns, despotism, 'cui ex honesto nulla est spes',* will tolerate no other master; and when it speaks, there is neither integrity nor duty to consider, and the blindest obedience is the sole virtue remaining to slaves.

This is the final stage of inequality, the extreme point that closes the circle and links up with the point from which we set out. Here, all individuals become equal again because they are nothing, here subjects have no law save the will of the master, nor the master any rule save that of his passions, and here the notions of the good and principles of justice once more evaporate. Here, everything is brought back solely to the law of the strongest, and hence to a new state of nature differing from the one with which we began in that the one was the state of nature in its pure form and the other the fruit of excessive corruption. There is so little difference, moreover, between the two states, and the despot so fully dissolves the contract of government that he remains master only as long as he is the strongest; when he is driven out, he has no right to protest against violence. The outbreak that ends with the garroting or dethronement of a sultan is just as lawful an act as those by which he, shortly before, held sway over the lives and property of his subjects. Force alone main-

tained him; force alone overthrows him. All things happen
according to the natural order, and whatever the result of
these brief and frequent revolutions, no one can complain of
the injustice of others, but only of his own carelessness or
misfortune.

In thus discovering and tracing the lost and forgotten
paths that must have led men from the natural state to the
civil state, in reconstructing, together with the intermediate
positions I have just noted, those which a lack of time has led
me to omit or which imagination has not suggested, no
attentive reader can fail to be impressed by the formidable
distance that separates these two states. He will see in this
slow succession of things the solution to an infinity of moral
and political problems that philosophers cannot unravel. He
will understand that because the human race of one era is not
the human race of another, Diogenes could not find a man
because he searched among his contemporaries for a man
from a time that no longer was. Cato, he will say, perished
with Rome and freedom, for he was not of his century, and
this greatest of men could only astound the world he would
have ruled five centuries earlier. In short, the attentive reader
will explain how, through gradual degeneration, the soul
and the human passions change their nature, so to speak;
why in the long run our needs and our pleasures change
their objects; and why, because original man gradually dis-
appeared, society offers to philosophers' eyes only an assem-
blage of spurious men and artificial passions produced by
all men's new relations and lacking a true foundation in
nature. What reflection teaches about this is fully confirmed
by observation: savage man and civilized man differ so much
in the depths of their hearts and in their inclinations that
what constitutes the supreme bliss of the one would drive the
other to despair. The savage man breathes only peace and
freedom; he wishes only to live and remain idle, and even the
serenity of the Stoic does not approach his profound indifference toward every other object. The ever-busy civilized man,
in contrast, sweats, scurries about, and constantly frets in
search of ever more laborious occupations; he toils until
death, and even hastens toward his grave in getting ready to

live, or surrenders his life to acquire immortality. He pays court to great men he loathes and rich men he holds in contempt; he spares nothing to gain the honour of serving them; he delightedly boasts of his own humble station and of their protection, and, proud of his slavery, he speaks patronizingly of those who have not the honour of sharing it. What a spectacle for a Carib would be the trying and envied labours of a European minister! How many cruel deaths would that indolent savage not prefer to the horrors of such a life, which often is not even sweetened by the pleasure of doing good? For him to understand the motives of anyone assuming so many cares, he would have to assign some meaning to the words 'power' and 'reputation'; he would have to learn that there is a class of men who set some value on the gaze of the rest of the world, and who can be happy and content with themselves on the testimony of others rather than on their own. Such is indeed the cause of all these differences: the savage lives within himself; the social man, outside himself, lives only in the opinion of others and it is, so to speak, from their judgement alone that he gets the sense of his own existence. It is not my purpose here to show how this disposition gives rise to so much indifference toward good and evil coupled with such fine moralistic talk, or how, because everything is reduced to appearances, everything comes to be sham and put on—honour and friendship, virtue, and often even vices themselves in which one eventually discovers the secret of glorying; or show how as a result of always asking others what we are and never daring to wonder about this ourselves in the midst of so much philosophy, humanity, good manners, and sublime maxims, we have only deceptive and frivolous façades, honour without virtue, reason without wisdom, and pleasure without happiness. It is enough for me to have proved that this is not at all the original state of man, and that only the spirit of society and the inequality it engenders transforms and corrupts in this way all our natural inclinations.

I have endeavoured to set out the origin and progression of inequality, the establishment and abuse of political societies, in so far as these things can be deduced from the nature of man by the light of reason alone, independently of the sacred dogmas that give sovereign authority the sanction of divine right. It follows from this description that inequality, being almost non-existent in the state of nature, derives its strength and growth from the development of our faculties and the progress of the human mind, and eventually becomes stable and legitimate through the institution of property and laws. It also follows that moral inequality, authorized by positive law alone, is contrary to natural right whenever it is not matched with physical inequality—a distinction that adequately determines what we should think of the form of inequality that prevails among all civilized peoples—for it is manifestly contrary to the law of nature, however it is defined, that a child should rule over an old man, that an idiot should guide a wise man, and that a handful of men should gorge themselves with superfluities while the starving multitude goes in want of necessities.

NOTES

A Herodotus* relates that after the murder of the false Smerdis, the seven liberators of Persia gathered to deliberate the form of government they would give the state. Otanes vigorously urged a republic: a remarkable opinion for a satrap since, over and above the claim he might have to the empire, great men fear more than death a type of government that forces them to respect men. Otanes, as might be expected, was not heeded, and seeing that they were proceeding toward the election of a monarch, he who wanted neither to obey nor to command voluntarily yielded his right to wear the crown to the other contenders, asking in return only that he and his descendants be free and independent. This was granted him. Even if Herodotus did not inform us of the restriction placed on this privilege, it would be necessary to assume it; otherwise Otanes, not recognizing any sort of law and not being accountable to anyone, would have been all-powerful in the state, more powerful than the king himself. In a case like this, however, there was little likelihood that a man capable of being content with such a privilege would abuse it. Indeed, there is no evidence that this right ever caused the kingdom the slightest trouble, either from the wise Otanes or from any of his descendants.

B From the outset, I confidently rely on one of those authorities who are respected by philosophers because they speak from a solid and sublime reason that philosophers alone know how to discover and recognize:

Whatever interest we may have in knowing ourselves, I wonder if we do not know better everything that is not ourselves. Supplied by nature with organs designed uniquely for our preservation, we use them only in order to receive impressions of external things; we seek only to reach beyond ourselves and exist outside ourselves; too much concerned to multiply the functions of our senses and to increase the outward extent of our being, we seldom make use of that inner sense that reduces us to our true dimensions, and separates us from all that is not part of us. Nevertheless, this is the sense that we must use if we wish to know ourselves; it is the only one by which we can judge ourselves. But how can this sense be activated and given its full range? How can we purge our soul, where it resides, of all the mind's illusions? We have lost the habit of using this sense; it has remained unexercised amid the tumult of our physical sensations, dried up by the fires of our passions; the heart, the mind, the senses—all have worked against it. Buffon, *Histoire naturelle*, iv. *De la Nature de l'Homme*, 151.*

C The changes in man's conformation that may have been produced by the long-established practice of walking on two feet, the similarities still seen between his arms and the front legs of quadrupeds, and the inferences drawn from their way of walking, have given rise to doubts about the way that must have been the most natural for us. Every child begins by crawling on all fours and requires our example and our lessons to learn how to stand upright. There are even savage nations like the Hottentots who, being very neglectful of their children, let them walk on their hands for so long that later it is hard to get them to straighten up; the children of the Caribs in the West Indies do the same. There are various instances of quadruped men; and I could cite among others the case of the child discovered in 1344, near Hesse, who had been nursed by wolves, and who said afterwards at the Court of Prince Henry that if the choice had depended on him alone, he would rather have gone back to the wolves than to have lived among men. He had become so accustomed to walking like those animals that it was necessary to tie wooden splints to him to force him to stand erect and keep his balance on two feet. The same is true of the child found in 1694 in the forests of Lithuania, who had lived among bears. He gave no sign of reason, says M. de Condillac*; he walked on all fours, had no language, and uttered sounds that in no way resembled those of a man. The little savage of Hanover who was taken several years ago to the English Court had all the trouble in the world making himself walk on two feet, and in 1719 two other savages found in the Pyrenees ran about the mountains in the manner of quadrupeds. As for the possible objection that this means depriving man of the use of his hands to which we owe so many advantages, I would answer that the example of monkeys, beyond showing that hands can well be used in both ways, merely proves that man can put his limbs to more useful purposes than those of nature, and not that nature has destined man to walk differently from the way it teaches him.

It seems to me that there are far better reasons, however, for saying that man is a biped. First, even if we are shown that he could first have been formed differently from the way we now see him and yet have in the end become what he is, this would not be enough to conclude that that is what actually happened: for after demonstrating the possibility of such changes, it would still be necessary, before accepting them, to show at least their likelihood. Moreover, though human arms were apparently able to serve as legs if need be, that is the lone observation in favour of this hypothesis, as against many that conflict with it. The chief of these are: that the way in which a man's head is attached to his body, instead of directing his eyes to the horizon like those of all other animals, and as he himself does when he walks erect, would have kept him in walking on all fours with his eyes fixed straight at the ground, a condition hardly conducive to the individual's preservation; that the tail he lacks and of which he has no need in walking on two feet, is useful to quadrupeds and none of them is without one; that the breast of a woman, very well placed for a biped who holds her infant in her arms, would be so poorly placed for a quadruped that none has it located there; that the length of the human hindquarters being excessive in proportion to the forelegs (which means crawling on our knees when walking on all fours) the whole would have made for an animal that is ill-proportioned and awkward in walking; that if he had set his foot down flat as well as his hand, he would have had one less joint in his hind leg than the other animals, namely the one that joins the cannon-bone to the tibia; that in setting down only the tip of his foot, as he would undoubtedly have been forced to do, the tarsus (not to mention the several bones that make it up) would appear to be too large to take the place of the cannon-bone, and its articulations with the metatarsus and the tibia too close together to give the human leg in this position the same flexibility as those of quadrupeds. The example of infants is taken from an age when their natural strength is not yet developed nor the limbs toned up and so proves nothing, and I could as well say that dogs are not destined to walk because for several weeks after birth they only crawl. Particular facts have very little force against the universal practice of all men, even of nations that, having had no communication with other ones, could not have imitated them. A child abandoned in the forest before he learned to walk, and suckled by some beast, would have followed the example of his nurse in learning to walk like her; habit could have given him abilities he did not acquire from nature; and just as persons without arms succeed, with practice, in doing with their feet whatever we can do with our hands, he will finally succeed in using his hands as feet.

D Should my readers include a scientist sufficiently ill-informed to raise objections concerning this assumption of this natural fertility of the earth, I shall answer him with the following passage:

Because plants get for their nourishment much more substance from air and water than they get from the earth, it happens that when they rot, they return more to the earth than they have taken from it; furthermore, a forest keeps the waters of the rain by preventing evaporation. Thus in a wood left untouched for a long time, the layer of soil that supports vegetation would increase considerably; but because animals return less to the earth than they draw from it, and men consume enormous quantities of timber and plants for fires and other uses, it follows that in an inhabited country the layer of vegetative soil must always diminish and eventually become like the soil of Arabia Petraea, and so many other provinces of the Orient, which is in fact the area of most ancient habitation, where today we find only salt and sand; for the fixed salts of plants and animals remain, while all the other particles are volatilized. (M. de Buffon, *Hist. Nat.*)*

To this may be added the factual proof based on the great number of trees and plants of every species that blanketed nearly all the uninhabited islands discovered in recent centuries, and what history tells us about the huge forests all over the earth which had to be cut down as it became populated and civilized. On this I will make three remarks. First, if there is a form of vegetation that can make up for the destruction of vegetable matter by animals, according to M. de Buffon's argument, it is primarily the wooded areas, the treetops and leaves of which collect and absorb more water and moist air than do other plants. Secondly, the destruction of the topsoil—that is, the loss of the substance suited to vegetation—must accelerate in proportion to the earth's degree of cultivation and to the consumption of its products of every kind by its more industrious inhabitants. My third and most important remark is that the fruits of the trees provide the animal with a more abundant supply of food than can the other plants: an experiment I myself performed by comparing the productivity of plots of ground equal in size and quality, one covered with chestnut trees and the other sown with wheat.

E Among the quadrupeds, the two most universal distinguishing features of the carnivorous species are the shape of the teeth and the conformation of the intestines. Herbivorous animals all have blunt teeth, like the horse, cattle, sheep, and the hare. The carnivores' teeth, however, are pointed, like the cat, the dog, the wolf, and the fox. As for the intestines, the frugivores have some, like the colon, that are not found in carnivorous animals. It therefore appears that man, having teeth and intestines like the frugivores, should naturally be placed in this class,* and not only do anatomical observations confirm this opinion, but the monuments of antiquity lend it considerable support. 'Dicaerchas', says St Jerome, 'relates in his books on Greek antiquities that during the reign of Saturn, when the earth was still fertile by itself, no man ate flesh, but all lived off the fruits and vegetables that grew naturally.' (*Against Jovinianus*, II. 13.)†

† This opinion is further substantiated by reports of several modern travellers. Among others, François Coréal* testifies that most of the inhabitants of the Lucayes, transported by the Spaniards to the islands of Cuba, Santo Domingo, and elsewhere, died as a result of eating meat. *Added 1782.*

One may see from this how I overlook many points I could use to bolster my argument. Since prey is almost the only thing carnivores fight over, and since frugivores live together in constant peace, it follows that if the human race were of the latter kind, then it would clearly have had an easier time living in the state of nature and much less need and many fewer opportunities for leaving it.

F   All knowledge that requires reflection, all knowledge that is acquired only by the association of ideas and is perfected only over time, seems altogether beyond the savage man's reach, owing to the absence of communication with his fellow man, that is, to the absence of an instrument to use for such communication, and the absence of needs that make it necessary. His knowledge and skills are limited to leaping, running, fighting, throwing stones, and climbing trees. And though these things are all he knows, he has in return a much better knowledge of them than do we who have less need of them; and because these skills depend entirely on bodily training and cannot be transmitted or further developed from one person to another, the first man could have been as skilful as the last of his descendants.

Travellers' reports are full of examples of the strength and vigour of men in barbarian and savage nations; no less do these travellers praise the savages' dexterity and nimbleness; and since all that is needed to observe these things are eyes, there is no reason why we should not believe the testimony of eyewitnesses, from which I draw several random examples from the first books that come to hand. Kolben says:

The Hottentots are better at fishing than the Europeans of the Cape. They are similarly skilled with the net, the hook, and the barb, in coves as in rivers. They are no less adroit at catching fish by hand. They are incomparably adept swimmers. Their style of swimming is startling and peculiar to them. They swim with their bodies upright and their arms held up out of the water so that they look as if they are walking on land. In the roughest seas when the waves form so many mountains around them, they dance, as it were, on the crests of the waves, rising and falling like a cork.*

'The Hottentots', the same author continues, 'are surprisingly agile in hunting, and their fleetfootedness surpasses the imagination.' He is surprised that they do not more often put their agility to bad use, which does in fact sometimes happen, as we can tell from an example he gives:

A Dutch sailor disembarking at the Cape engaged a Hottentot to follow him to the town with a cask of tobacco weighing about twenty pounds. When they were some distance from the crew, the Hottentot asked the sailor if he knew how to run. 'Run?' answered the Dutchman, 'Yes, quite well.' 'We shall see,' replied the African and, racing off with the tobacco, he vanished from sight in a trice. The sailor, bemused by such amazing speed, did not think of making chase, and never saw his tobacco or his porter again.

They have such quick sight and a hand so unerring that Europeans do not even come close to them. At a hundred paces they will throw a stone and hit a mark the size of a halfpenny, and what is even more surprising is that instead of fixing their eyes on the mark as we do, they make continual movements and contortions. It looks as if their stone was borne by an invisible hand.

Father du Tertre* says much the same thing about the savages of the West Indies as I just quoted about the Hottentots of the Cape of Good Hope. He especially praises their accuracy in using arrows to shoot birds on the wing or fish in the water, which they then catch by diving. The savages of North America are no less famous for their strength and dexterity, and here is an example that allows us to judge that of the Indians of South America:

In 1746, an Indian from Buenos Aires, after being condemned to the galleys of Cadiz, proposed to the governor that he win back his freedom by risking his life at a public festival. He pledged that he would attack by himself the most enraged bull with nothing in hand but a rope, that he would ground the animal, seize it with his rope by whatever part he was told, saddle it, bridle it, mount it, and fight two other of the most furious bulls to be let out of their pen, and kill them, one after the other, the moment he was bid to do so, without anyone's help. His request was granted, and he was true to his word, managing to do everything he had pledged. As for the way he performed, and for all the details of the encounter, see the first volume (in—12°) of M. Gautier's* *Observations sur l'histoire naturelle*, page 262, from which this story was taken.

G M. de Buffon says:

The lifespan of horses is, as in all other species of animals, proportional to the amount of time they take to complete their growth. Man, who takes fourteen years to grow up, can live six or seven times as long as this period, that is, ninety or a hundred years; the horse, whose growth is completed in four years, can live six or seven times as long as that, or twenty-five or thirty years. Cases that might depart from this rule are so rare that they ought not to be regarded as exceptions from which conclusions could be drawn; and just as large horses reach their full growth in less time than lighter horses, so they have a shorter lifespan and are old by the age of 15.*

H I think there is another difference between carnivores and frugivores, one even more universal than that mentioned in note E, since this one also applies to birds. The difference consists in the number of young, which never exceeds two in each litter among the herbivores, but usually exceeds that number among voracious* animals. It is easy to learn nature's intentions in this regard from the number of teats, which is only two for each female of the first kind, the mare, the cow, the goat, the doe, the ewe, and so forth, and which is always six or eight in the other females, such as the dog, the cat, the wolf, the tigress, and the like. The hen, the goose, and the duck, which are all voracious birds (as are the eagle, the sparrowhawk, and the owl), also brood over a large number of eggs, which never happens with the pigeon, the turtledove, or other birds that eat nothing but seeds, and hardly ever lay and brood over more than two eggs at a time. The reason that can be given for this difference is that animals that live only on herbs and plants, grazing nearly all day and forced to spend a great deal of time feeding themselves, would not be up to the suckling of several young ones, whereas voracious animals, taking their meals almost in an instant, can more readily and frequently return to their young and the hunt, and make up for the loss of such a large quantity of milk. On all this there are many particular observations and reflections to be made, but this is not the place for them; and it is enough for me to have shown in this section the most general system of nature, a system that provides a further reason for removing man from the class of carnivorous animals and putting him among the frugivorous species.

I   A celebrated author,* adding up the goods and the evils
of human life, compared the two sums and concluded that
the evils greatly outweighed the good, that all in all life was a
rather wretched gift to man. I am not at all surprised by his
conclusion; he based his whole argument on the constitution
of civilized man. If he had gone back to natural man, we may
predict that he would have come up with very different
results; he would have realized that man has hardly had any
evils other than those he has inflicted on himself, and that
nature would have been vindicated. It is not without difficulty that we have managed to make ourselves so unhappy.
When we consider, on the one hand, man's colossal achievements, so many sciences developed, so many arts invented,
so many forces exploited, chasms filled over, mountains pul-
verized, rocks broken up, rivers made navigable, land cleared,
lakes carved out, swamplands drained, enormous buildings
erected on land, the sea bespread with ships and sailors; and
when, on the other hand, we search with a little meditation
for the real advantages that have accrued from all this for the
happiness of the human race, we cannot fail to be struck by
the stunning disproportion between these things, or fail to
deplore man's blindness, which to feed his lunatic vanity and
I know not what undue self-admiration, makes him fervently
chase after all the miseries of which he is capable, and which
a beneficent nature had painstakingly kept from him.

Men are wicked; doleful and constantly repeated experience spares us of any need of proof for it; yet man is naturally
good, as I believe I have demonstrated. What then can so
have perverted him, if not the changes that have come about
in his constitution, the progress he has made, and the knowledge he has gained? Admire human society as you will, it is
no less true that it necessarily leads men to abominate each
other to the degree that their interests conflict, and to pretend
to render each other services while in fact doing each other
every imaginable harm. What is one to think of dealings in
which each private individual's reason dictates maxims flatly
contrary to those that the public reason preaches to the
society as a whole, and in which each person profits from the
misfortunes of others? There may be no well-off man whose

death is not secretly wished by his grasping heirs, often his own children; no ship at sea whose wreck would not be welcome news for some merchant; no place of business that some debtor[†] would not like to see burn up with all its papers in it; no nation that does not gloat at the disasters of its neighbours. This is how we each find our profit at the expense of our fellows; and one man's loss is nearly always someone else's gain. What is even more dangerous, however, is that public disasters are looked forward to and hoped for by a multitude of individuals. Some wish for diseases, others death, others war, and still others famine. I have seen despicable men weep with sorrow at the prospect of a good harvest; and the deadly Great Fire of London, which claimed the lives and possessions of so many ill-fated victims, made the fortunes perhaps of more than ten thousand persons. I know that Montaigne* blames the Athenian Demades for having had punished a worker who sold coffins at a very high price and so profited from the death of citizens, but the reason that Montaigne cites, namely that everyone should have been punished, clearly validated my argument. Let us therefore break through all our insincere displays of benevolence, look at what goes on in the depths of our hearts, and reflect on what the state of things must be where all men are forced both to fawn on and destroy each other, and where duty makes them enemies and interest makes them manipulative swindlers. If I were told that society is so constituted that each man gains by serving others, I should reply that that would all be very well but for the fact that he gains even more by harming them. No profit is so legitimate that it cannot be surpassed by what can be done illegitimately, and a harm done to a neighbour is always more lucrative than any good turn. All that remains is the problem of finding ways to ensure one's impunity, and that is the end to which the powerful turn all their drive and the weak all their guile.

Savage man, when he has eaten, is at peace with all nature and the friend of all his fellows. Does a dispute sometimes arise over a meal? He will never come to blows about this

[†] of bad faith   *Added 1782.*

without his first comparing the difficulty of winning with that of finding his sustenance elsewhere, and because the struggle involves no vanity, it ends after a few fisticuffs; the victor eats, the vanquished goes off to seek better luck, and all is peaceful. Things are very different, however, with man in society; first comes the matter of providing the necessities, and then the superfluities; next come pleasures, then enormous wealth, then subjects, and then slaves; man in society does not have a moment of respite. What is most remarkable is that the less natural and urgent the needs, the more the passions increase and, what is worse, so does the power to satisfy them; so that after a long period of prosperity, and after devouring many treasures and afflicting many men, my hero will end up slitting every throat until he is the sole master of the universe. Such is the abbreviated moral portrait, if not of human life, at least of the secret designs in the heart of every civilized man.

Compare with an open mind the condition of the civilized man with that of the savage, and observe, if you can, how—aside from his wickedness, his needs, and his miseries—civilized man has opened new doors to suffering and death. If you consider the mental agonies consuming us, the violent passions exhausting and crushing us, the inordinate toil with which the poor are burdened, and the even more dangerous laxness to which the rich abandon themselves, so that the former die of their needs while the latter die of their over-indulgences; if you think of the monstrous concoctions they eat, their harmful seasonings, their corrupt foods, and adulterated drugs; the trickery of those who sell such things and the errors of those who administer them, of the poison in the vessels* in which they are prepared; if you take note of the epidemic diseases generated by the bad air in places where masses of men are gathered together, the diseases occasioned by the complexity of our way of life, by our moving back and forth between the interiors of houses and the open air, by the use of clothes put on or taken off with too little precaution, and all the solicitudes that our excessive sensuality has turned into necessary habits and whose neglect or deprivation then costs us our life or our health; if you also take into account fires that consume, and earthquakes that crush, whole cities, wiping out their inhabitants by the thousands; in short, when you add up the dangers that all these causes endlessly heap over our heads, you will see how dearly nature makes us pay for the contempt we have shown for its lessons.

I shall not repeat here what I have said elsewhere on the subject of war,* but I wish that educated men would for once desire or dare to tell the public the details of the horrors committed by contractors of military supplies and hospitals. We would see their none-too-secret manœuvres make the most brilliant armies dissolve into less than nothing and cause the death of more soldiers than are cut down by the enemy's steel. It is no less staggering to count the men engulfed by the sea every year, whether by hunger, scurvy, pirates, fire, or shipwrecks. We must ascribe to the institution of property, and hence to society, murders, poisonings, highway robberies, and even the punishments for those crimes— punishments required to forestall still greater evils, but that, for every murder, cost the lives of two or more men and so in fact double the loss to the human species. How many shameful steps are there for preventing human birth and outwitting nature? Whether by those coarse and depraved tastes that insult her most charming work, tastes unknown to savages or animals, and that arise in civilized countries only out of corrupt imaginations; whether by secret abortions, fit products of debauchery and perverted honour; whether by the exposure and murder of hosts of infants, victims of their parents' poverty or the cruel shame of their mothers, or by the mutilation of those unfortunates in whom a part of their existence and all their posterity are sacrificed for the sake of some worthless songs, or, worse still, sacrificed to the brutal jealousy of a few men; in this last case, this mutilation doubly offends nature, both in the treatment received by the victims and the use to which they are destined.†

---

† But are there not cases, a thousand times more frequent and dangerous, where paternal rights openly offend humanity? How many talents are suppressed and inclinations forced by the unwise constraint of fathers! How

What if I undertook to show the human race attacked at its very source and even in the most sacred of all bonds, where one dares not listen to nature until one has consulted fortune, and where, with civil disorder confounding virtues and vices, sexual continence becomes a criminal precaution and the refusal to grant one's fellow being his life an act of humanity? But without ripping away the veil that conceals so many horrors, let us be content to point out the evil for which others must supply the remedy.

When one adds to all this the numbers of unwholesome trades that shorten lives or destroy men's vigour—trades like working in mines, processing metals and minerals, especially lead, copper, mercury, cobalt, arsenic, realgar,* together with those other dangerous trades that daily cost the lives of many workers, including roofers, carpenters, or masons, or labourers in quarries—if one sums up, I say, all these negative things, then we can see in the establishment and improvement of societies the explanation for the diminution of the species that has been observed by more than one philosopher.

A taste for luxury, which is impossible to check in men greedy for their own conveniences and for esteem from others, soon completes the evil that societies begin, and

many men would be distinguished in the right situation but die unhappy and dishonoured in another situation for which they have no taste! How many happy but unequal marriages* have been broken or disturbed, and how many faithful wives dishonoured by an arrangement of circumstances that is always contrary to nature! How many other bizarre unions are formed by interest and disavowed by love and reason! How many even honest and virtuous spouses torment each other just because they are ill-matched! How many young and unhappy victims of their parents' greed descend into vice or spend their grim days weeping, groaning in unbreakable bonds that the heart rejects and that gold alone has formed! Happy sometimes are those whose courage and even whose virtue delivers them from life before a barbarous violence drives them to crime or despair. Forgive me, ever-lamenting father and mother; it is with regret that I embitter your sufferings; but may it serve as an eternal and terrible example to anyone who dares, in the very name of nature, to violate the most sacred of its rights!

If I have spoken only of those ill-formed marriages that are the handiwork of our civilization, is it to be thought that those over which love and sympathy have presided are without their disadvantages? *Added 1782.*

under the pretence of providing a livelihood for the poor (who should not have been made so in the first place), it impoverishes everyone else and sooner or later depopulates the state.

Luxury is a remedy much worse than the evil it claims to cure, or rather it is itself the worst of evils in any state, whether small or large; and to feed the crowds of lackeys and poor people it creates, luxury crushes and ruins the farmer and the townsman. It is like those torrid southern winds that, blanketing the grass and foliage with ravenous insects, deprive productive animals of their subsistence and bring famine and death wherever they blow.

From society and the luxury it begets arise the liberal and mechanical arts, commerce, literature, and all the superfluities that make industry flourish and enrich and destroy states. The reason for this deterioration is very simple. It is easy to see that agriculture by its nature is bound to be the least lucrative of all arts because its products are the most indispensable for all men and hence must fetch a price proportional to the reach of the poorest. From the same principle we can derive the rule that in general the arts are lucrative in inverse proportion to their usefulness, and the most necessary are bound in the end to be the most neglected. We thereby see what must be considered the true advantages of industry and the actual results of its advances.

Such are the observable causes of all the miseries to which the most esteemed nations are driven by opulence. As industry and the arts spread and thrive, the farmer, who is scorned, burdened with the taxes needed to maintain luxury, and condemned to divide his life between labour and hunger, abandons his fields to seek in the towns the bread he ought to be bringing there. The more the capital cities dazzle the admiring, wide-eyed people, the more one must bemoan the sight of the derelict countryside, the land lying fallow, and the highways overrun with unfortunate citizens turned beggars or thieves, fated someday to end their misery on the rack or a dungheap. That is how the state grows rich on the one hand, and feeble and depopulated on the other, and how the most powerful monarchies, after much effort to make themselves opulent and uninhabited, end up the prey of poor nations that succumb to the fatal temptation to invade them, only to enrich and enfeeble themselves in turn until they too are invaded and destroyed by others.

Would somebody be so kind as to explain to us, for once, what could have produced those hordes of barbarians who for so many centuries swarmed over Europe, Asia, and Africa? Did they owe their sizeable population to their industry and arts, the wisdom of their laws, or the excellence of their political system? Let the learned kindly tell us why, far from multiplying to such an extent, these fierce and brutish men, without ideas, without restraint, without education, did not slay each other in perpetual combat over their grazing- or hunting-ground? Let our scholars explain how these wretches even had the effrontery to look in the eye such clever men as we were, with such fine military discipline, such fine codes, and such wise laws? Why is it that after society was perfected in the countries of the North and great pains had been taken to teach men their reciprocal duties and the art of living pleasantly and peaceably together, we see coming from them nothing like the great numbers of men whom it once produced. I fear that it will occur to someone to answer that men wisely invented all these great things— the arts, sciences, and laws—as a therapeutic plague to preclude the excessive increase of the species, for fear that this world, which is destined for us, might in the end become too small for its inhabitants.

What?* Must societies be destroyed, the 'mine' and 'yours' abolished, and men return to the forests to live with the bears? A conclusion typical of my opponents, which I would rather obviate than allow them the shame of drawing it. O you, to whom the heavenly voice has not made itself heard, and who acknowledge no other destiny for your species than to end this fleeting life in peace; you who can leave your lethal acquisitions, your troubled minds, your corrupt hearts, and your frantic desires in the midst of cities, reclaim—since it is up to you to do so—your ancient and earliest innocence; go into the woods, lose the sight and memory of the crimes of your peers, and have no fear of demeaning your species by renouncing its enlightenment in order to renounce its vices.

As for men like me, whose passions have for ever shattered their original simplicity, who can no longer subsist on herbs and nuts, nor do without laws and leaders; those whose first father was honoured with supernatural lessons, those who can see in the intention of giving from the very beginning a morality to human actions that they would otherwise not have acquired for a long time the reason for a maxim indifferent in itself and inexplicable in any other system;* in short, those who are convinced that the divine voice called the whole human race to the enlightenment and happiness of celestial intelligences; all those will try, by practising the virtues that they obligate themselves to perform as they learn to understand them, to deserve the eternal prize they must expect for it; they will respect the sacred bonds of the societies of which they are members; they will love their fellow men and serve them with all their might; they will scrupulously obey the laws and the men who are the authors and ministers of the laws; above all, they will honour the good and wise princes who can prevent, cure, and relieve the host of abuses and evils that are ever ready to overwhelm us; they will sustain the ardent devotion of these worthy rulers, in showing them without fear or flattery the greatness of their task and the strictness of their duty, but they will none the less despise a constitution that can be maintained only with the help of numerous estimable persons more often wished for than found, and from which, in spite of their attentions, always arise more real calamities than seeming benefits.

J   Among the men we know, whether from our own or the accounts of historians or travellers, some are black, others white, others red; some wear their hair long, others have only woolly curls; some have hair all over, others not even a beard. There were, and possibly still are, peoples of gigantic size, and disregarding the fable of the pygmies, which may well be just an exaggeration, we know that the Laplanders and particularly the Greenlanders are well below the average height of man. It is even claimed that there are whole peoples with tails like quadrupeds, and without giving blind credence to the accounts of Herodotus and Ctesias,* one can at least extract from them this very probable opinion: if one could have made solid observations in ancient times when various peoples' ways of life differed from each other much more than they do today, much more conspicuous variety in the shapes and structure of the body would have been noted. All these facts, which are easily provided with incontestable proofs, could surprise only those who are accustomed to looking merely at the objects around them and who are unaware of the powerful effects of the differences in climates, air, foods, ways of living, habits in general, and especially the startling effects of the same causes acting repeatedly over a long succession of generations. Nowadays, when trade, travel, and conquests bring various peoples closer together, and when their ways of life become ever more alike through frequent communication, one notices that certain national differences have diminished, and everyone can see, for example, that the French of today no longer have the tall, blond, fair-skinned bodies described by the Roman historians, although time, together with the intermingling of Franks and Normans, themselves fair and blond, should have restored what frequent contact with the Romans may have done to reduce the influence of the climate on the population's natural constitution and complexion. All these observations on the variety that a thousand causes can produce, and indeed have produced, in the human species, lead me to wonder whether the various animals resembling man and taken by travellers without close scrutiny to be beasts, either because of a few differences they observed in external conformation or simply because these animals did not speak, might not indeed be genuine savage men, whose race, scattered in the forests since antiquity, with no chance to develop any of its potential faculties, had not achieved any measure of perfection, and remained in the primitive state of nature. Let me give an example of what I mean.

According to the translator of *Histoire des voyages,**

In the Kingdom of the Congo, one finds many of those large animals that are called orang-utans in the East Indies, and which stand roughly midway between the human species and baboons. Andrew Battel* relates that in the forests of Mayomba in the forest of

Loango, one sees two sorts of monsters, the larger of which are called 'pongos'* and the smaller ones 'enjokos'. The former bear an exact resemblance to man, but they are much heavier and very tall. Together with a human face, they have deep-set eyes. Their hands, cheeks, and ears are hairless except for their eyebrows, which are very long. Although the rest of their body is rather hirsute, this hair itself is not very thick and it is brown in colour. Finally, the only feature that distinguishes them from men are their legs, which have no calves. They walk upright, with a hand on the hair of another's neck; their lair is in the forest; they sleep in the trees, and there they make a sort of roof that shelters them from the rain. Their food consists of fruits or wild nuts. They never eat meat. The custom of the Negroes passing through the forests is to light fires during the night. They notice that when they depart in the morning, the pongos gather around the fire, and do not go away until it has died out; for with all their dexterity, they do not have enough sense to keep the fire going by adding more wood to it.

They sometimes walk in troops and kill Negroes making their way through the forests. They even fall on elephants coming to graze in the places where they live, and they harass them so much with their fists or sticks that they force them to go away bellowing. Pongos can never be taken alive because they are so strong that ten men would not be enough to hold one; but the Africans take many young ones after killing the mother, to whose body the young cling tenaciously. When one of these animals dies, the others cover the corpse with a pile of branches or foliage. Samuel Purchas adds that in his conversation with Andrew Battel, he learned how a pongo abducted a little Negro, who spent a whole month in the society of these animals, for they do no harm to men they surprise, at least so long as those men pay them no attention, as the little Negro had done. Battel did not describe the second species of monster.

Dapper* confirms that the Kingdom of the Congo is full of these animals that bear in the East Indies the name of 'orang-utans', which means 'inhabitants of the woods' and which the Africans call 'quojas-morros'. This beast, he says, is so like a man that several travellers have entertained the idea that it could be the issue of a woman and an ape—an idle fancy that the Negroes themselves dismiss. One of these animals was shipped from the Congo to Holland and presented to Prince Frederick-Henry of Orange. It was as tall as a 3-year-old child and less than perfectly healthy, but sturdy and well-proportioned, very agile and lively, with chunky and muscular legs, the whole front of its body hairless, but the back covered with black fur. At first glance, its face resembled that of a man, but its nose was flat and snubbed; its ears were also those of the human species; its breast—for it was a female—was plump, its navel deep-set, its shoulders nicely articulated, its hands divided into fingers and thumbs, its calves and heels thick and fleshy. It often walked upright on its legs; it was able to lift and carry fairly heavy objects. When it wanted to drink, it took the lid off the pot with one hand, and held the base with the other. Afterwards it gracefully wiped its lips. It lay down to sleep, its head on a pillow, covering itself with such dexterity that one would take it for a human in bed. The Negroes tell strange stories about this animal. They not only declare that it takes women and girls by force, but that it dares to attack armed men. In short, there is much to suggest that it is the satyr of the ancients. Merolla* may have been talking of just these creatures when he records that the Africans on the hunt sometimes catch savage men and women.

The third volume of this same *Histoire des voyages* contains more about these species of anthropomorphic animals under the names 'beggos' and 'mandrills'. To confine ourselves to the preceding accounts, we find in the descriptions of these supposed monsters striking similarities to the human species and fewer differences from men than those one could find between one man and another. It is not clear in these passages why the writer withholds the name of savage men from the animals in question, but one may readily guess that the reason is their stupidity and also the fact that they did not speak—poor reasons for those who know that although the organ of speech is natural to man, speech itself is not natural to him, and who recognize how much his perfectibility may have raised the civilized man above his original state. The brevity and poverty of these descriptions allow us to judge how inadequately the animals were observed and by what preconceived assumptions they were glanced over. For example, they are pronounced monsters, yet it is conceded that they reproduce themselves.* In one place Battel says the pongos kill Negroes passing through the forests; in another, Purchas says they do them no harm even when they surprise them, at least so long as the Negroes pay them no attention. The pongos gather around fires started by Negroes and, when the latter go off, go away in turn when the fire goes out; there is the fact—now let us read the observer's commentary: 'For with all their dexterity, they do not have enough sense to keep the fire going by adding more wood to it.' I would like to guess how Battel, or Purchas, his compiler, could have known that the departure of the pongos was due to their stupidity rather than their will. In a climate like that of Loango, a fire is not imperative for animals, and if the Negroes light one, it is less to ward off the chill than to frighten away predatory animals. Thus, it is quite understandable that after enjoying the flames for a while and getting thoroughly warmed, the pongos grow bored with staying continually in the same place, and head off to forage for food, which requires more time than if they ate meat. Furthermore, we know that most animals, and man is no exception, are naturally lazy, and take no more pains than absolutely necessary. Finally, it seems very odd that the pongos, whose dexterity and strength are admired, who know how to bury their dead and who construct roofs of branches, would not know how to throw logs on a fire. I myself have seen a monkey perform this very act of which the pongos are supposed to be incapable; it is true that at the time I was not addressing this question and hence I committed the same error for which I am criticizing the travellers: I failed to consider whether the monkey's intention was in fact to keep the fire going or, as I now think, to imitate a human act. But whatever the case may be, it has been amply demonstrated that the monkey is not a variety of man, not only because it is deprived of the faculty of speech, but above all because we are sure that this species does not have the faculty of perfecting itself, which is the specific characteristic of the human race. No sufficiently careful experiments seem to have been done with the pongo and the orang-utan for us to draw the same conclusion. There is, however, one means by which, if the orang-utan and others were of the human species, the most cursory of observers could even demonstrably assure themselves of this;* but beyond the fact that such an experiment would involve more than a single generation, it must be judged impracticable, for what is only a supposition would have to be shown to be true before the experiment that was to prove it true could be tried innocently.

Hasty judgements that are not the fruit of enlightened reason are apt to run to extremes. Our travellers simply make the beasts bearing the names 'pongos', 'mandrills', and 'orang-utans' into the same creatures that the ancients, using the names 'satyrs', 'fawns', and 'sylvans', made into divinities. It may be that after more exact research, it will be found that they are[†] men. In the mean time, it seems to me that in this matter we have as much reason to heed Merolla—a learned monk and eyewitness who, all for all his candour and simplicity, was no less a man of intelligence—as we do the merchant Battel, or Dapper, or Purchas, and the other compilers of books.

What judgement would these observers have made about the child found in 1694, of whom I have spoken earlier, a child who gave no sign of reason, walked on all fours, had no language, and made vocal noises that in no way sounded human? According to the philosopher[*] who related these facts to me, it was a long time before the child could pronounce a few words, and he did this crudely. As soon as he was able to speak, he was questioned about his earlier condition, but he could remember no more of it than we can remember what happened to us in the cradle. If, unluckily for him, this child had fallen into the hands of our travellers, we cannot doubt that after noting his silence and stupidity, they would have decided to send him back into the forest or lock him up in a menagerie, after which in their brilliant accounts of their travels, they would have learnedly spoken of him as a most curious beast somewhat resembling a man.

Despite the two or three hundred years since the inhabitants of Europe have been pouring into other parts of the world and constantly publishing new collections of voyages and travel, I am persuaded that the only men we know are the Europeans; what is more, it appears from the absurd preconceptions that have not died out even among men of letters, that every author writes under the pompous title of the study of man only a study of the men of his own country. However much individuals come and go, it seems that philo-

[†] neither beasts nor gods, but *Added 1782.*

sophy does not travel, so true is it that the philosophy of
one nation is ill-suited for another. The cause of this is
obvious, at least in the case of distant countries. There are
scarcely more than four sorts of men who go on long-distance
voyages: sailors, merchants, soldiers, and missionaries. Now
it can hardly be expected that the first three kinds would
prove good observers, and as for the fourth, taken up with
the sublime vocation to which they have been summoned,
even if they are not subject to the same prejudices of station
as are all the others, one must believe that they would not
willingly take up research that would look like a matter of
simple curiosity and divert them from the more important
work on which they have set their sights. Furthermore, to
preach the Gospel effectively, one needs only zeal and God
supplies the rest; but to study man, one needs to have abilities
that God does not commit himself to grant anyone and are
not always the lot of saints. One does not open an account of
travels without coming upon descriptions of characters and
customs, but one is altogether astounded to find that these
writers who describe so many things tell us only what everyone already knew, and could see at the other end of the
world only what they could see without leaving their own
street, and that the true features that differentiate nations,
and that strike eyes made to see them, have almost always
escaped their notice. From this has come that fine ethical
adage so often repeated by the philosophy-enamoured throng:
that men are the same everywhere, and since they all have
the same passions and vices, it is rather pointless to seek to
characterize different peoples—which is just about as well
thought-out as to say that Pierre and Jacques are indis-
tinguishable, since they both have a nose, a mouth, and two
eyes.

Shall we never see reborn those happy times when peoples
did not take it into their heads to 'philosophize', but when a
Plato, a Thales, or a Pythagoras, smitten with a burning
desire for knowledge, undertook the most extensive voyages
solely to learn, and travelled far in order to shake off the
yoke of national prejudices, to get to know men by their re-
semblances and their differences, and to gain some universal

knowledge that does not exclusively belong to one century or one country, but being that of all times and all places, is, so to speak, the universal science of the wise?

We admire the munificence of several men whose curiosity has led them to undertake, or underwrite, costly expeditions to the Orient with learned men and artists, to make drawings of ruins or to decipher and copy inscriptions; but I find it hard to imagine why in a century that prides itself on its remarkable knowledge, we do not find two well-matched men, both rich—one in money and the other in genius—both prizing glory and aspiring to immortality, one of whom would sacrifice twenty thousand crowns of his fortune and the other ten years of his life, to make a historic voyage around the world in order to study, not the sempiternal plants and stones, but for once men and customs, and who, after all the centuries spent measuring and appraising the house, should finally decide that they would like to know about its inhabitants.

The academicians who have travelled to the northern parts of Europe and the southern part of America have gone to visit those places more in the role of surveyors than as philosophers. However, since some have been both, we cannot regard as entirely unknown the regions observed and described by men like La Condamine* and Maupertuis. The jeweller Chardin, who travelled like Plato, has left nothing more to be said about Persia; China seems to have been well observed by the Jesuits. Kaempfer gives a tolerable idea of the little he saw of Japan. Apart from these accounts, we know nothing of the people of the East Indies, toured by Europeans wholly engrossed with filling their purses rather than their heads. The whole of Africa with its multitudinous inhabitants, as distinctive in their character as in their colour, has yet to be studied. The whole world is bespread with peoples about whom we know only their names, and we go about judging the whole human race! Suppose a Montesquieu, a Buffon, a Diderot, a Duclos, a D'Alembert, a Condillac, and other men of that stamp were to travel in order to instruct their countrymen, observing and describing as only they know how, Turkey, Egypt, Barbary, the Empire of Morocco,

Guinea, the land of the Kaffirs, the interior and the east coast of Africa, the Malabars, Mongolia, the banks of the Ganges, the kingdoms of Siam, Pegu and Ava,* China, Tartary, and especially Japan; and then in the other hemisphere, Mexico, Peru, Chile, and the lands by the Straits of Magellan, not forgetting the Patagonians, true and false, Tucamán,* Paraguay if possible, Brazil; and finally the Caribbean islands, Florida, and all the savage countries—the most important voyage of all, and the one that would have to be undertaken with the greatest possible assiduity. Suppose that, on their return from these memorable journeys, these new Hercules then wrote at leisure the natural, moral, and political history of what they had seen, we ourselves would see a new world issue from their pen, and we would thereby learn to know our own. If such observers as these were to say of one animal that it is a man and of a different animal that it is a beast, then I say we must believe them; it would be most simple-minded, however, to accept the authority of uncultured travellers about whom one is sometimes tempted to ask the very question that they take it upon themselves to answer in the case of other animals.

K   All this seems manifestly clear to me, and I cannot imagine where our philosophers locate the source of all the passions they attribute to natural man. Apart from the physically necessary demanded by nature itself, all our other needs are such only through habit, prior to which they are not needs at all, or through our desires, and one does not desire what one is not in a position to know of. Whence it follows that since the savage man desires only the things he is acquainted with and knows only the things within his reach or easy to acquire, nothing should be so tranquil as his soul and nothing so narrow as his mind.

L   I find in Locke's *Of Civil Government** an objection that seems to be too specious* for me be able to cover it over:

The end of association between male and female being not barely procreation but the continuation of the species, this association betwixt male and female ought to last, even after procreation, so long as is necessary to the nourishment and support of young ones, who are to be sustained by those that begot them, till they be able to shift and provide for themselves. This rule, which the infinite wise Maker hath set to the works of his hands, we find the inferior creatures steadily obey. In those viviparous animals which feed on grass, the association between male and female lasts no longer than the very act of copulation; because the teat of the female being sufficient to nourish the young till it be able to feed on grass, the male only begets, but concerns not himself for the female or young, to whose sustenance he can contribute nothing. But in beasts of prey the association lasts longer, because the female, not being able well to subsist herself and nourish her numerous offspring by her own prey alone, a more laborious as well as more dangerous way of living than feeding on grass, the assistance of the male is necessary to the maintenance of their common family, if one may use that term, which cannot subsist till they are able to prey for themselves, but by the joint care of male and female. The same is to be observed in all birds (except some domestic ones where plenty of food excuses the male from feeding and taking care of the young brood) whose young needing food in the nest, the male and female continue mates till the young are able to use their wings and provide for themselves.

And therein I think lies the chief, if not the only reason, why the male and female in mankind are tied to a longer association than other creatures. The reason is that the woman is capable of conceiving, and *de facto* is commonly with child again, and brings forth, too, a new birth long before the former is out of dependency for support on his parents' help and able to shift for himself, and has all the assistance that is due to him from his parents. Thus, because the father, who is bound to take care of those he hath begot, is under obligation to continue in conjugal society with the same woman longer than other creatures, whose young being able to subsist for themselves before the time of procreation returns again, the conjugal bond dissolves of itself, and they are at liberty, till Hymen at his usual anniversary season summons them again to choose their mates. Wherein one cannot but admire the wisdom of the great Creator, who having given to man foresight, and an ability to lay up for the future, as well as to supply the present necessity, hath made it necessary that the society of man and wife should be more lasting than that of male and female amongst other creatures; that so their industry might be encouraged and their interest better united, to make provision and lay up goods for their common issue, which uncertain mixture or easy and frequent dissolutions of conjugal society would mightily disturb.

The same love of truth that has prompted me to present this objection in all sincerity prompts me to make a few further observations, if not to answer it, at least to clarify it.

1. First, I note that moral proofs are without great force in scientific matters and that they serve more to explain existing facts than to establish the real existence of those facts. This is the kind of proof Locke uses in the passage just cited; for although it might be advantageous to the human race if the union of man and woman were permanent, it does not follow that it has been so established by nature; otherwise we should have to say that nature had also instituted civil society, the arts, commerce, and everything else supposedly beneficial for mankind.

2. I do not know where Locke discovered that the society of male and female lasts longer among predatory animals than among those that live on grass, or that the male among them helps the female to feed the young, for we do not see that dogs, cats, bears, or wolves appreciate their female better than horses, rams, stags, or any other quadrupeds recognize theirs. On the contrary, it seems that if the male's help were necessary to the female to sustain her young, this would be particularly true of the species that live only on grass, because the mother needs much time for grazing, and because all that time she is forced to ignore her brood, while a female bear or wolf can devour her prey in an instant, thus allowing her all the more time, without going hungry, to suckle her young. My argument is confirmed by an observation of the relative number of teats and offspring that distinguishes the carnivorous from the frugivorous species, of which I spoke in note H. If that observation is correct and universal, the fact that a woman has only two teats and rarely gives birth to more than one child at a time provides one more powerful reason for doubting whether the human species is naturally carnivorous. Thus, to arrive at Locke's conclusion, we would have to turn his argument upside down. Nor is the distinction any more sound when applied to birds. For who could be assured that the union of male and female is more lasting among vultures and ravens than among turtledoves? We have two species of domestic birds, the duck and the pigeon,

that provide us with clear counterexamples to Locke's system. The pigeon, which feeds only on grain, stays together with its female, and the couple work jointly to feed their young. The duck, whose voracity is well known, recognizes neither its female nor its young, and has no share in their sustenance. And among chickens, a species hardly less voracious, we do not see the rooster go to any trouble over the brood. If in some other species, the male shares with the female the care of feeding the young, it is because birds, which cannot fly at first and whose mother cannot suckle them, are much less able to do without the father's help than are quadrupeds, for whom the mother's teat suffices, at least for a while.

3. There is much uncertainty about the principal fact serving as the basis of Locke's whole argument; for to know whether, as he claims, in the pure state of nature the woman is typically pregnant again and gives birth to yet another baby long before the previous one is able to fend for himself, experiments would have to be done that Locke assuredly did not do and that no one is in a position to do. The constant living together of husband and wife is a situation so conducive to a new pregnancy that it is difficult to believe that chance encounters or sexual impulse alone would produce effects as frequent in the pure state of nature as in the state of conjugal society: such longer spells between childbearing might tend to make the children more robust and might also be rewarded by having the ability to conceive last to a more advanced age among women who had exploited it less when young. As for children, there are many reasons for believing that their strength and their organs develop later among us than they did in the primitive state of which I speak. The original weakness that children owe to their parents' constitution, the care taken to swaddle and restrict all their limbs, the softness in which children are reared, and perhaps the use of a milk other than their mother's—all these thwart and delay in them the first progress of nature. The diligence they are obliged to apply to a thousand things to which their attention is constantly drawn while their physical faculties go unexercised, may further significantly hamper their growth; hence, if instead of at first overburdening and tiring their minds in a thousand ways, their bodies could get exercised

by the constant movements that nature seems to expect them to do, we may believe that they would be able to walk, act, and fend for themselves much earlier.

4. Finally, Locke proves at the very most that there might well be a motive for the man to stay attached to the woman while she has a child, but he in no way proves that the man must have been attached to her before the birth and during the nine months of pregnancy. If this woman is of no interest to the man for these nine months, if indeed she becomes a stranger to him, why should he help her after the birth? Why would he help her to raise a child he does not know is his and whose birth he neither desired nor foresaw? Locke clearly assumes what is in question: for the issue is not why the man should remain attached to the woman after the birth, but why he becomes attached to her after the conception. Once his appetite is satisfied, the man no longer has any need for a particular woman, nor the woman for a particular man. The man has not the least concern, nor perhaps the least idea, of the consequences of his act. The man goes off in one direction, the woman in another, and it is unlikely that at the end of nine months either will remember ever knowing the other—for the kind of memory by which one individual is more attracted to another for the procreative act requires, as I show in the text, more progress or more corruption in the human understanding than can be ascribed to the state of animality that is at issue here. Thus, another woman can satisfy a man's new desires just as serviceably as can the woman he has previously known, and another man similarly satisfy the woman, assuming she was moved by the same urge during pregnancy, which may reasonably be doubted. If, however, in the state of nature the woman no longer experiences the passion of love after conceiving the child, the obstacle to her society with the man thus becomes even greater, for she has no longer any need of either the man who impregnated her or of any other. Hence the man has no reason to seek out the same woman, nor the woman to seek the same man. Locke's argument thus collapses, and all his dialectic has not saved him from the error committed by Hobbes and others. They had to explain a fact about the state of nature, that is, a state where men

lived in isolation and where one particular man had no reason to stay close by another man, nor perhaps men a reason to live close by other men, which is much worse; and it did not occur to these philosophers to look back across the centuries of society, that is, beyond times when men have always a reason to live close to one another, and when a particular man has often a reason to live close to a particular man or woman.

M I shall take care not to embark on the philosophical reflections that might be made on the advantages and disadvantages of this institution of languages: I would not be the one to be granted leave to attack common errors; and the educated are too attached to their prejudices to suffer my supposed paradoxes with patience. Therefore, let those speak who have not committed the crime of sometimes daring to side with reason against the opinion of the multitude:

Nec quidqum felicitati humani generis decederet, pulsa tot linguarum peste et confusione, unam artem callerent mortales, et signis, motibus, gestibusque licitum foret quidvis explicare. Nunc vero ita comparatum est, ut animalium quae vulgo bruta creduntur, melior longe quam nostra hac in parte videatur conditio, ut pote quae promptius et forsan felicius, sensus et cogitationes suas sine interprete significent, quam ulli queant mortales, praesertim si peregrino utantur sermone. (Isaac Vossius).*

N Plato, showing how ideas of what we call integers and their relations are necessary to the lesser arts, rightly mocks the writers of his time who claimed that Palamedes invented numbers during the siege of Troy, as if, says the philosopher,* Agamemnon might until then have been unaware how many legs he had. Indeed, we realize the impossibility of society and the sciences having reached the stage they were in at the time of the siege of Troy without mens' having had the use of numbers and arithmetic. But the fact that a knowledge of numbers is needed before other knowledge can be acquired does not make it any easier to imagine how numbers were invented; once their names are known, it is easy to explain their meaning and to evoke the ideas that these names represent; but in order to invent them, it would be necessary before conceiving these same ideas, to be, so to speak, accustomed to philosophical meditations, to be practised in considering entities in their essence and independently of all other perception, an act of abstraction that is very difficult, very metaphysical, and somewhat unnatural, but without which these ideas could never be transmitted from one species or genus to another, nor could numbers become universal. A savage could consider his right leg and his left leg separately, or view them together under the indivisible idea of a pair without ever thinking that he had two of them; for the representative idea depicting an object for us is one thing and a numerical idea specifying an object is another. Still less could he count up to five, and even though by putting his hands together he could see that the fingers matched exactly, he was still far from thinking of their numerical equality. He had no more knowledge of how many fingers he had than he did of the number of the hairs on his head, and if someone, after first getting him to understand what numbers are, then told him that he had as many toes as fingers, he might have been very surprised, in comparing them, to discover that this was true.

O   One must not confuse vanity [*amour-propre*] and self-love [*amour de soi-même*], two very different passions in their nature and in their effects. Self-love is a natural sentiment that prompts every animal to watch over its own preservation and that, guided in man by reason and modified by pity, produces humanity and virtue. Vanity is only a relative, artificial sentiment born in society, a sentiment that prompts each individual to set greater store by himself than by anyone else, that triggers all the evil they do to themselves and others, and that is the real source of honour.

This being well understood, I will say that in our primitive state, in the true state of nature, vanity does not exist; for since each individual regards himself as the sole spectator by whom he is observed and the sole creature in the world who takes an interest in him, it follows that a sentiment that originates in comparisons he is incapable of making could not develop in his soul. For the same reason, this man could feel neither hatred nor the desire for vengeance, passions stemming only from a belief that some offence has been received; and because it is the contempt or the intention to hurt, and not the harm itself that constitutes the offence, men who do not know how to appraise one another or compare themselves with one another, can do one another much violence, when it brings them some advantage, without ever giving offence to one another. In short, every man, looking upon his fellow men hardly differently from the way he regards animals of another species, can snatch the prey of the weaker, or yield his own to the stronger, without envisaging these thefts as anything but natural occurrences, without the least stirring of arrogance or spite, and with no other passion but the joy of success or the pain of failure.

P It is an extremely remarkable fact that after the many years spent by Europeans agitating themselves about converting the savages of the various countries of the world to their way of life, they have so far been unable to win over a single one, not even with the help of Christianity, for our missionaries sometimes make Christians of them, but never civilized men. Nothing can overcome the savages' unconquerable revulsion at the prospect of embracing our morals and style of life. If these poor savages are as unhappy as they are claimed to be, by what unimaginable perversity of judgement do they consistently refuse to govern themselves in imitation of us or learn to live happily among us, whereas one reads in a thousand places that Frenchmen and other Europeans have voluntarily taken refuge among these peoples, spent their whole lives there without being able to quit such a strange way of life, and we see sensible missionaries tenderly lamenting calm and innocent days spent among these much despised peoples? To the suggestion that savages are insufficiently enlightened to make sound judgements about their own condition or ours, I would reply that the assessment of happiness is less the business of reason than of feeling. Besides, that answer can be turned against us with even more force, for there is a greater distance between our ideas and the frame of mind required to imagine the savages' taste for their way of life than between the ideas of savages and the frame of mind required for them to imagine ours. Indeed, after a few observations they can readily see that all our labours are directed toward only two goals: namely the comforts of life for oneself and esteem from others. But how are we to imagine the kind of pleasure a savage takes in spending his life alone in the depths of the woods, or fishing, or blowing into a bad flute without ever managing to produce a single note from it or troubling to learn how to do so?

On a number of occasions savages have been brought to Paris or London or other cities; people hastened to spread before them our luxury, our riches, and all our most useful and singular arts, none of which has ever provoked them to anything but wide-eyed admiration, without the least stirring of desire for possession. I remember among others the story of a North American chief who was brought to the Court in England some thirty years ago. A thousand things were put before his eyes in quest of a present that would please him, but nothing could be found that seemed to interest him. He appeared to find our weapons heavy and cumbersome; our shoes hurt his feet, our clothes cramped him; he rejected everything. At length, it was noticed that having picked up a woollen blanket, he seemed to enjoy wrapping it around his shoulders. 'You would at least agree', someone promptly said to him, 'that this article is useful?' 'Yes,' he replied, 'it seems to me almost as good as an animal skin.' He would not have said even that if he had worn them both in the rain.

Someone might tell me that habit makes everyone attached to his own way of life, and thus prevents the savage from perceiving what is good in ours. According to this argument, it must seem extraordinary that habit proves stronger in preserving the savages' taste for their misery than the Europeans' enjoyment of their felicity. But to meet this objection with an unimpeachable response—without mentioning all the young savages we have unsuccessfully attempted to civilize, without speaking of the Greenlanders and inhabitants of Iceland whom people attempted to educate and feed in Denmark, and who all died of sorrow and despair, either from wasting away or drowning in the sea when they tried to swim back home—I shall be content to cite a single, well-attested example, which I submit to the scrutiny of admirers of European political order:

All the efforts of the Dutch missionaries at the Cape of Good Hope have never been able to convert a single Hottentot. Van der Stel, governor of the Cape, having taken in one as a baby, had him reared in the principles of the Christian religion and the practice of European customs. He was richly dressed, taught several languages, and his progress matched the care taken in his upbringing. The governor, full of high hopes based on the boy's intelligence, sent him to India with a commissioner-general who employed the boy usefully in the company business. He returned to the Cape on the commissioner's death. A few days after his return, while he was visiting some of his Hottentot kinsmen, he decided to strip off his European finery and clothe himself in a sheepskin. He returned to the fort in this new garb, carrying a package that contained his former clothes, and presenting them to the governor, he made the following speech: 'Kindly observe, sir, that I disown this apparel for good. I also disown the Christian religion for the rest of my life. My resolution is to live and die in the religion, customs, and usages of my ancestors. The one favour I ask of you is to allow me to keep the necklace and the cutlass I am wearing. I shall keep them for the love of you.' Immediately, without waiting for Van der Stel's reply, he took to his heels to escape and was never again seen at the Cape.*

Q One might object that amid such disorder men, instead of stubbornly slaughtering each other, would have scattered if there had been no boundary to impede their dispersal. In the first place, however, these boundaries would at least have been those of the world; and when we think of the excessively large population that results from the state of nature, we shall conclude that, in that state, the earth would soon be bespread with men, forced to remain together. Moreover, they would have scattered if the evil had been swift or had it been a change happening overnight; but they were born under the yoke and already were in the habit of bearing it when they came to feel its weight, and they were content to wait for the chance to shake it off. Finally, already accustomed to a thousand conveniences that forced them to remain together, dispersal was no longer as easy as in early times when no one needed anyone but himself and everyone made up his mind without waiting for the approval of another.

R Field Marshal de V——* recounted that during one of his campaigns, owing to the excessive frauds of a supply-contractor that caused distress and grumbling in the army, he heartily rebuked the man and threatened to have him hanged. 'The threat does not bother me,' replied the scoundrel brazenly, 'and I am most pleased to tell you that they do not hang a man who's worth a hundred thousand crowns.' 'I do not know how it turned out,' added the marshal in all candour, 'but in fact the man was not hanged, though he deserved it a hundred times over.'

S Distributive justice would even oppose that strict equality found in the state of nature, were it practicable in civil society, and because all members of the state owe it services commensurate with their strength and abilities, the citizens in turn should be singled out and favoured in proportion to their services. It is in this sense that we should interpret a passage in Isocrates* where he praises the early Athenians for their ability to discern the more advantageous of the two sorts of equality, one of which consists of allotting the same benefits to all citizens impartially and the other of distributing them according to each one's merit. These adept politicians, adds the orator, by banishing that unjust equality that makes no distinction between wicked and good people, steadfastly stood by the equality that rewards and punishes everyone according to his merit. In the first place, however, there has never been a society, no matter what degree of corruption it may have reached, in which no distinction has been made between wicked and good people, and in matters of morals where the law cannot lay down sufficiently precise guidelines to serve as a rule for the magistrate, the law, in order not to leave the fate or station of citizens to his discretion, very wisely forbids him to judge persons and allows him to judge only actions. Only morals as pure as those of the ancient Romans can endure censors, and among us such tribunals would soon have overturned everything. It is for public esteem to distinguish between wicked and good men. The magistrate is the judge only of what is strictly law; the people are the true judge of morals—an honest and even enlightened judge on this point, sometimes deceived but never corrupted. The station of citizens thus should be regulated not according to their personal merit, which would leave the magistrate with the means of applying the law more or less arbitrarily, but according to the real services that they render the state, which admit of more exact measurement.

EXPLANATORY NOTES

3 *Sovereign Lords*: the formal title given to the members of Geneva's Conseil Général, composed of all the republic's citizens (about 1,500 men out of a total population of roughly 20,000). In dedicating his book to the republic, Rousseau addresses himself to them and not to the magistrates of the Petit Conseil, referred to below as 'Magnificent and Most Honoured Lords', who wielded effective power in the city. After composing the *Discourse*, Rousseau won reinstatement of his own citizenship, which he had lost after a youthful conversion to Catholicism in Turin.

5 *mists of time*: a partially autonomous bishopric in the Middle Ages, Geneva became a Protestant republic during the Reformation.

7 *recognized*: by the Treaty of Turin in 1754.

9 *virtuous citizen*: Isaac Rousseau (1672–1747), a watchmaker. In 1722 he exiled himself to neighbouring Nyon after a quarrel that brought him trouble with Geneva's authorities. Rousseau, whose mother Suzanne Bernard (1673–1712) had died giving birth to him, was left in the care of his uncle.

10 *inhabitants*: resident aliens in Geneva, without rights of citizenship.

unfortunate events: tension between the ruling patrician families and citizens who wanted the General Council to exercise more effective power had erupted into serious conflict in 1737. An Edict of Mediation, brokered by France the following year, reaffirmed the Petit Conseil's control over legislative initiative.

11 *destiny*: Genevan women were not themselves citizens and were excluded from political participation.

14 *Delphi*: 'Know Thyself'.

Glaucus: Plato, *Republic*, 10. 611.

16 *Burlamaqui*: Jean-Jacques Burlamaqui (1694–1748), prominent Genevan exponent of natural rights theories, to whose *Principes du droit naturel* (Geneva, 1747) Rousseau refers (ch. 1, § 2).

16 *law of nature*: Rousseau uses this expression sometimes to mean 'natural law' (a system of moral norms), and sometimes to designate the physical laws of nature, including man as an amoral or premoral being.

17 *sociability*: a key concept for some natural rights theorists, notably Pufendorf, as well as for Rousseau's friend Diderot. Rousseau divorces self-preservation from sociability.

19 *Disce*: 'Learn what God has ordered you to be, and what your place is in human affairs.' Persius, *Satires*, iii. 71–3.

24 *facts*: the biblical account of human origins, which Rousseau, to avoid religious censure, prudently acknowledges to be true before setting it aside. But the phrase also suggests a broader contrast between facts in general and Rousseau's fictional portrait of the state of nature.

28 *fight*: Hobbes's views are somewhat different. See *De Cive*, i. 4 and *Leviathan*, ch. 13.

philosopher: Montesquieu, *The Spirit of the Laws*, i. 2. Richard Cumberland (1631–1738), bishop of Peterborough, whose *De Legibus naturae* (1670) is critical of Hobbes; Samuel Pufendorf (1632–94), a German natural rights theorist whose work was vastly influential throughout Protestant Europe. Rousseau had read Pufendorf's *De officio hominis et civis* (*On the Duty of Man and Citizen*, 1673) as a young man. He refers frequently in the *Discourse* to Pufendorf's major work, *De jure naturae et gentium* (*On the Law of Nature and Nations*, 1672), which he read in Jean Barbeyrac's annotated French translation (1712). References will be to the 1740 edition of this last, published as *Le Droit de la nature et des gens*.

29 *Coréal*: Francisco Coreal (1648–1708), Spanish explorer. Rousseau cites *Les Voyages de François Coréal aux Indes occidentales* (1722), i. 8.

30 *Plato*: *Republic*, 3, 405–6. Podalirius and Machaon: *Iliad*, 2. 731 f.

Celsus: A. Cornelius Celsus, first-century Roman encyclopaedist, author of several influential books on medicine.

31 *Laët*: Flemish explorer (1593–1649), who described an opossum in his *Histoire du nouveau monde*.

34 *perfectibility*: a neologism attributed to Turgot, and which Rousseau also uses in the sense of an open-ended process of

improvement, without any predetermined goal or achieved perfection.

35 *Indian*: Jean-Baptiste du Tertre (1610–87), *Histoire générale des Antilles, habitées par les Français* (1667), ch. 2.

37 *Condillac*: Etienne Bonnot, abbé de Condillac (1714–80), French philosopher, author of an *Essai sur l'origine des connaissances humaines* (1746) influenced by Locke. Rousseau also discusses his ideas about linguistic evolution in his *Essai sur l'origine des langues*, composed in the 1750s but published posthumously in 1781.

42 *public*: that is, usable as a means of reaching and convincing a broad and diverse audience.

43 *told*: by Pufendorf, *Droit*, ii, ch. 1, § 8; Hobbes, *Leviathan*, ch. 13.

44 *robust child*: Hobbes, *De Cive*, preface.

45 *virtutis*: 'So far has ignorance of vice been more advantageous to the Scythians than knowledge of virtue to the Greeks.' Justin, *Histories*, ii. 2.

recognize: Bernard Mandeville (1670–1733), in his *Fable of the Bees, or Private Vices Public Benefits* (expanded edition, 1723), a satirical poem followed by extensive remarks, including 'An Essay on Charity Schools', which contains an analysis of pity. See the edition by F. B. Kaye (Oxford, 1924), i. 254 ff.

46 *dedit*: 'Tenderness of heart is the gift Nature declares she gives to the human race with the gift of tears.' Juvenal, *Satires*, xv. 131–3. Most of this addition is taken from Rousseau's *Letter to d'Alembert* (1758).

47 *self-love*: *amour de soi*, linked to the instinct for self-preservation. Rousseau contrasts it with *amour-propre*, or vanity. See note (O) to the *Discourse*.

50 *Caribs*: Montaigne, *Essays*, i. 31.

61 *injury*: Locke, *An Essay concerning Human Understanding*, iv, 3, § 18. Locke actually says 'no injustice'. Rousseau's 'no injury' (*injure*) may be taken from an inaccurate quotation in Barbeyrac's introduction to Pufendorf. Whatever the case, Rousseau's emphasis on the psychological wound is significant.

64 *his own labour*: a traditional definition of justice. See Plato, *Republic*, i. 331e.

64 *labour*: Locke, *Two Treatises of Government*, II, § 27.

Grotius: Dutch jurist (1583–1645), in his *De jure belli ac pacis* (*On the Laws of War and Peace*, 1625), II, ch. 2, § 2. 'Thesmaphoria' derives from the Greek for 'law-bearing'.

67 *odit*: 'Shocked at a new-found evil, rich and yet wretched, he seeks to flee from his wealth, and hates what he once prayed for.' Ovid, *Metamorphoses*, xi. 127.

72 *fable*: probably La Fontaine's 'Le Vieillard et l'âne', vi. 8.

master: Pliny the Younger, *Panegyric of Trajan*, lv. 7.

Politicians: Rousseau's *politiques* includes writers on politics as well as statesmen. The 1782 text has 'our politicians' and 'our philosophers'.

mine: Herodotus, *Histories*, vii. 133–6. Rousseau changes the name of the speaker to that of the Spartan general Brasidas.

73 *appellant*: 'They call the most wretched servitude peace.' Tacitus, *Histories*, iv. 17. Like some other quotations in this part of the *Discourse*, it is slightly inaccurate, being drawn from the *Discourses concerning Government* (II, ch. 15) by the English republican Algernon Sidney (1622–83).

Locke and Sidney: the first of Locke's *Two Treatises on Government* and Sidney's *Discourses* are refutations of the absolutist thesis defended by Robert Filmer (1588–1653) in his *Patriarcha*, published in 1680.

74 *public good*: as Rousseau well knew, the *Traité des droits de la reine très chrétienne sur divers États de la monarchie d'Espagne* was published (anonymously) to support Louis XIV's territorial claims in the Netherlands rather than to acknowledge the king's submission to law. Diderot had recently cited the same text in the *Encyclopédie*, with a similar ironic awareness.

master: Pufendorf, *Droit*, VII, ch. 8, § 6, n. 2; Locke, *Two Treatises*, II, § 23.

75 *favour*: Pufendorf, *Droit*, VII, ch. 3, § 1.

76 *government*: in his *Social Contract*, Rousseau will denounce the 'common opinion' he follows here, asserting that only the agreement of the people among themselves to form a political association is a genuine contract. A relationship of mutual obligation between the people and its leaders does not have the same fundamental, deeply binding character.

78 *kings of kings*: a title used by the rulers of the Persian Empire.

81 *dextra*: 'If you should command me to bury my sword in the chest of a brother or the throat of a parent, or in the body of my wife heavy with child, I would perform it all, even if my right hand be unwilling.' Lucan, *Pharsalia*, i. 376–8, as given in Sidney, *Discourses*, ii. 19.

82 *spes*: 'In which there is no hope from an honest deed.' Tacitus, *Annals*, v. 3, as given in Sidney, *Discourses*, ii. 19.

86 *Herodotus*: *Histories*, iii. 80–3. The restriction was that Otanes should not violate the kingdom's laws.

87 *Buffon*: these are the opening lines of Buffon's discussion of man, the first part of his 'General History of Animals'. In the standard quarto edition of the *Histoire naturelle générale et particulière* (Paris, 1749–67), 15 vols., consulted for these notes, they appear at ii. 429–30.

   Condillac: *Essai sur l'origine des connaissances humaines*, I, iv, § 23.

89 *Buffon*: in his *Théorie de la terre*, the first section of the *Histoire naturelle*, i. 354–5.

90 *class*: this is one point on which Rousseau, who inclined to vegetarianism, disagreed with Buffon.

   Coréal: *Voyages aux Indes occidentales*, i. 2.

91 *cork*: Rousseau cites the Dutch traveller Peter Kolben's observations from the *Histoire générale des voyages*, a mid-eighteenth-century compilation edited by the abbé Prévost, v. 155–6.

92 *du Tertre*: *Histoire générale des Antilles*, ch. 1, para. 5.

   Gautier: Jacques Gautier d'Agoty (1710–85) was the editor of the periodical *Observations* (1752–8), i. 262.

93 *age of 15*: Buffon, *Histoire naturelle*, iv. 226–7.

   voracious: Rousseau uses this word variously to mean 'carnivorous' or 'omnivorous' and 'ravenous'. Characteristically, he links aggressive behaviour to meat-eating.

94 *author*: the French philosopher and scientist Maupertuis (1698–1759), in his *Essai de philosophie morale* (1749), ch. 2.

95 *Montaigne*: *Essais*, i. 22.

96 *vessels*: Rousseau (like some others of his day) believed that the use of copper pots was dangerous to human health.

97   *war*: *L'état de guerre*, in *Œuvres complètes*, iii. 601–16.

98   *realgar*: a kind of arsenic used by goldsmiths to enhance the look of their gold.

     unequal marriages: marriages between partners of different rank or class.

100 *What?*: this key paragraph was added by Rousseau when the *Discourse* was in page proofs.

101 *system*: probably a reference to God's injunction to Adam and Eve not to eat the fruit of the Tree of Knowledge.

     Ctesias: Persian physician at the court of Artaxerxes II, around 400 BC.

102 *voyages*: v. 87–9. What we call orang-outangs today are found in Sumatra and Borneo, not in Africa.

     Andrew Battel: (d. 1645), English merchant, whose travels were recorded by Samuel Purchas (1577–1626).

103 *pongos*: gorillas; the *enjokos* are unknown.

     Dapper: Olfert Dapper (d. 1670), Dutch physician and geographer.

104 *Merolla*: Jerome Merolla, seventeenth-century missionary to the Congo.

     reproduce themselves: 'monsters' (biological freaks) were supposed to be sterile.

105 *this*: an allusion to the possibility of cross-breeding. Buffon had proposed that a species be defined by the ability of its members to reproduce with each other.

106 *philosopher*: Condillac.

108 *La Condamine*: Charles-Marie de la Condamine (1701–74), French scientist, author of *Relation abrégée du voyage fait à l'intérieur de l'Amérique méridionale* (1745). Maupertuis, *Relation d'un voyage au fond de la Laponie* (1749). Jean Chardin (1643–1713), whose *Voyage en Perse et aux Indes orientales* (1686) was widely influential, notably on Montesquieu's *Lettres persanes* (1721). Engelbert Kaempfer (1651–1716), *History of Japan and Siam* (1728). Charles-Pinot Duclos (1704–72), author of *Considérations sur les mœurs de ce siècle* (1750).

109 *Pegu and Ava*: province and city in today's Myanmar.

     Patagonians: there were tales of huge men living in Patagonia at the tip of South America.

109 *Tucamán*: a part of Argentina.

Government: Locke, *Two Treatises*, II, § 79, 80. Rousseau is citing, with minor variations, a French translation which in turn deviates slightly from Locke's own text.

specious: in the old sense of attractive or plausible.

114 *Vossius*: 'It would in no way diminish the happiness of mankind if, banishing the deadly and confusing multiplicity of languages, all men were to cultivate one single and uniform art—and be able to express themselves on all subjects by means of signs, movements, and gestures. As things are, the condition of animals that the vulgar call beasts seems in this regard very much better than our own, for they make their feelings and thoughts understood more swiftly and perhaps more truly, without any distortion, and in this they are superior to men, especially men speaking a foreign language.' Where Rousseau has 'movements', Vossius has 'clues'.

philosopher: Plato, *Republic*, vii. 522.

118 *Cape*: *Histoire des voyages*, v. 175. The frontispiece of the original edition of the *Discourse* depicted this scene.

119 *V*: the duc de Villars (1653–1734), Marshal of France.

Isocrates: *Areopagetica*, 21–2.

THOMAS PAINE	**Rights of Man, Common Sense, and Other Political Writings**
JEAN-JACQUES ROUSSEAU	**The Social Contract** **Discourse on the Origin of Inequality**
ADAM SMITH	**An Inquiry into the Nature and Causes of the Wealth of Nations**
MARY WOLLSTONECRAFT	**A Vindication of the Rights of Woman**

JANE AUSTEN	**Emma**
	Mansfield Park
	Persuasion
	Pride and Prejudice
	Sense and Sensibility
MRS BEETON	**Book of Household Management**
LADY ELIZABETH BRADDON	**Lady Audley's Secret**
ANNE BRONTË	**The Tenant of Wildfell Hall**
CHARLOTTE BRONTË	**Jane Eyre**
	Shirley
	Villette
EMILY BRONTË	**Wuthering Heights**
SAMUEL TAYLOR COLERIDGE	**The Major Works**
WILKIE COLLINS	**The Moonstone**
	No Name
	The Woman in White
CHARLES DARWIN	**The Origin of Species**
CHARLES DICKENS	**The Adventures of Oliver Twist**
	Bleak House
	David Copperfield
	Great Expectations
	Nicholas Nickleby
	The Old Curiosity Shop
	Our Mutual Friend
	The Pickwick Papers
	A Tale of Two Cities
GEORGE DU MAURIER	**Trilby**
MARIA EDGEWORTH	**Castle Rackrent**

*The
Oxford
World's
Classics
Website*

www.worldsclassics.co.uk

- Information about new titles
- Explore the full range of Oxford World's Classics
- Links to other literary sites and the main OUP webpage
- Imaginative competitions, with bookish prizes
- Peruse the Oxford World's Classics Magazine
- Articles by editors
- Extracts from Introductions
- A forum for discussion and feedback on the series
- Special information for teachers and lecturers

www.worldsclassics.co.uk

MORE ABOUT **OXFORD WORLD'S CLASSICS**

American Literature

British and Irish Literature

Children's Literature

Classics and Ancient Literature

Colonial Literature

Eastern Literature

European Literature

History

Medieval Literature

Oxford English Drama

Poetry

Philosophy

Politics

Religion

The Oxford Shakespeare

A complete list of Oxford Paperbacks, including Oxford World's Classics, Oxford Shakespeare, Oxford Drama, and Oxford Paperback Reference, is available in the UK from the Academic Division Publicity Department, Oxford University Press, Great Clarendon Street, Oxford OX2 6DP.

In the USA, complete lists are available from the Paperbacks Marketing Manager, Oxford University Press, 198 Madison Avenue, New York, NY 10016.

Oxford Paperbacks are available from all good bookshops. In case of difficulty, customers in the UK can order direct from Oxford University Press Bookshop, Freepost, 116 High Street, Oxford OX1 4BR, enclosing full payment. Please add 10 per cent of published price for postage and packing.